MENTAL SUPERPOWERS

By Jan Hoek, clients from behavioral health of Kings County Hospital and other artists in various mental states

Why I believe that the ones with a different mind are the real Super Heroes of this planet.

me as a kid dressed like a homeless person

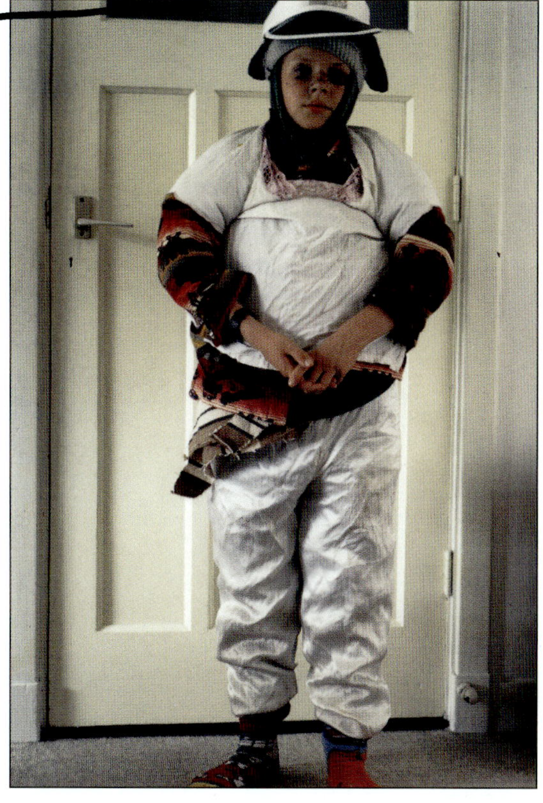

I've been drawn to society's outliers, the ones considered "crazy", since I was very young. I developed a belief that they had some kind of superpower other people didn't.

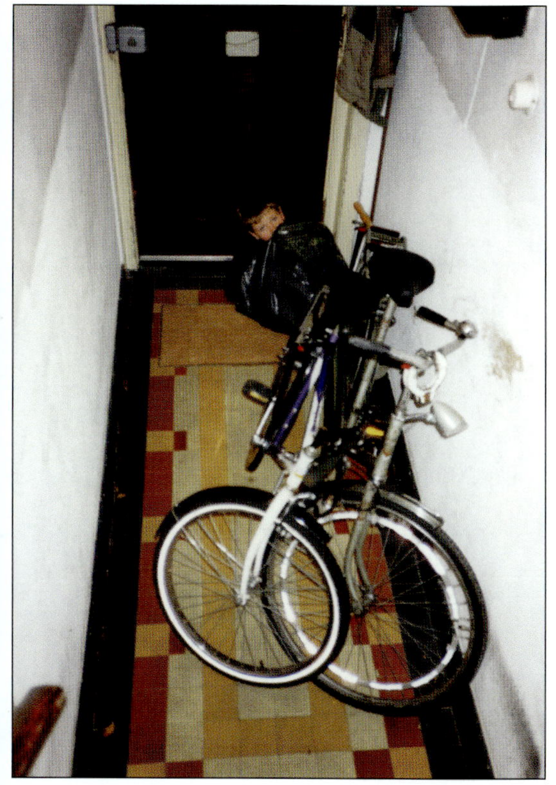

I remember that when I was a boy on the back of my mother's bike we passed by a bridge near central station and I saw a man coming out of his cardboard box.

He was wearing a hat made of leaves and cigarette stubs and the inside of his box, I saw, was adorned with porn and Christmas decorations. I wanted to become friends with him, but my mother wouldn't stop, and I was angry for days.

I've kept that tendency to romanticize those with a different wiring on the fringes of society, both as an artist and in my life in general, and that's why I can't help but see them as the world's real heroes.

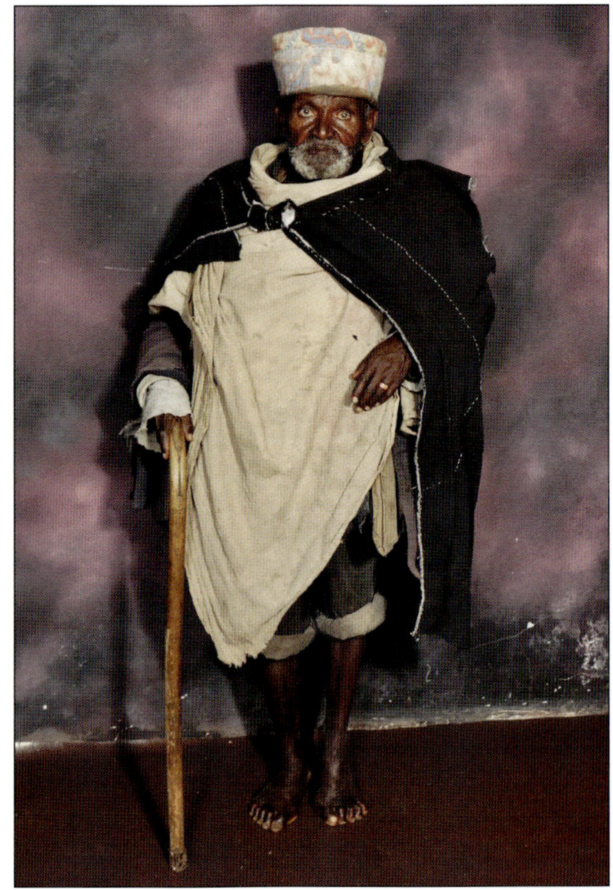

So I photographed troubled homeless men in Ethiopia who I saw as kings and emperors.

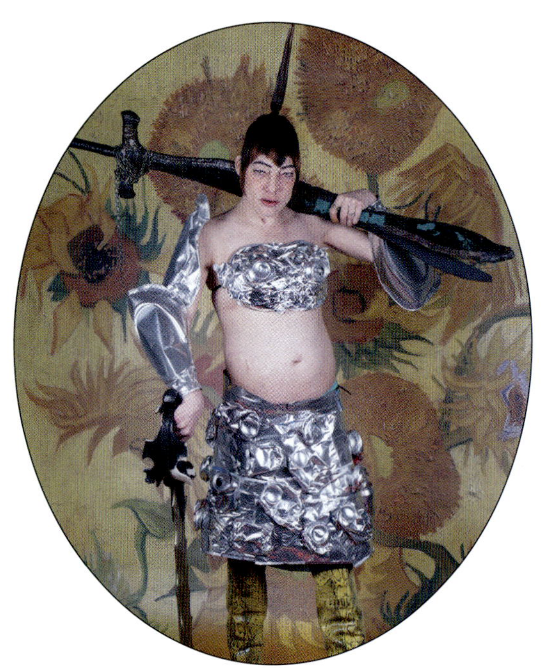

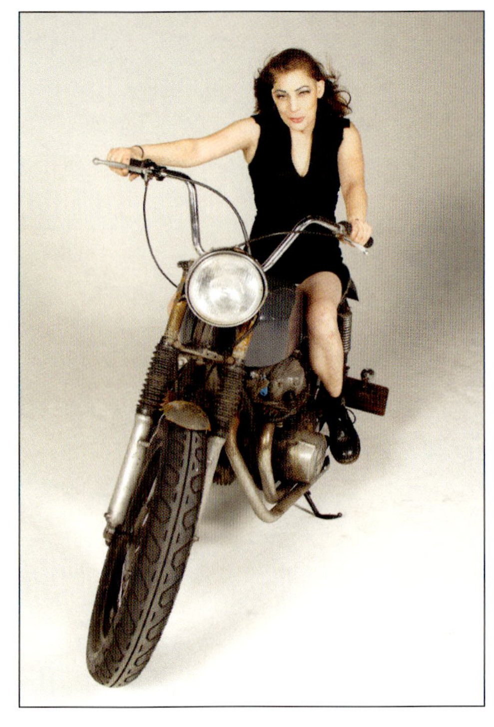

I photographed Kim, my muse, who had been addicted to heroin for 15 years but dreamed of being a supermodel

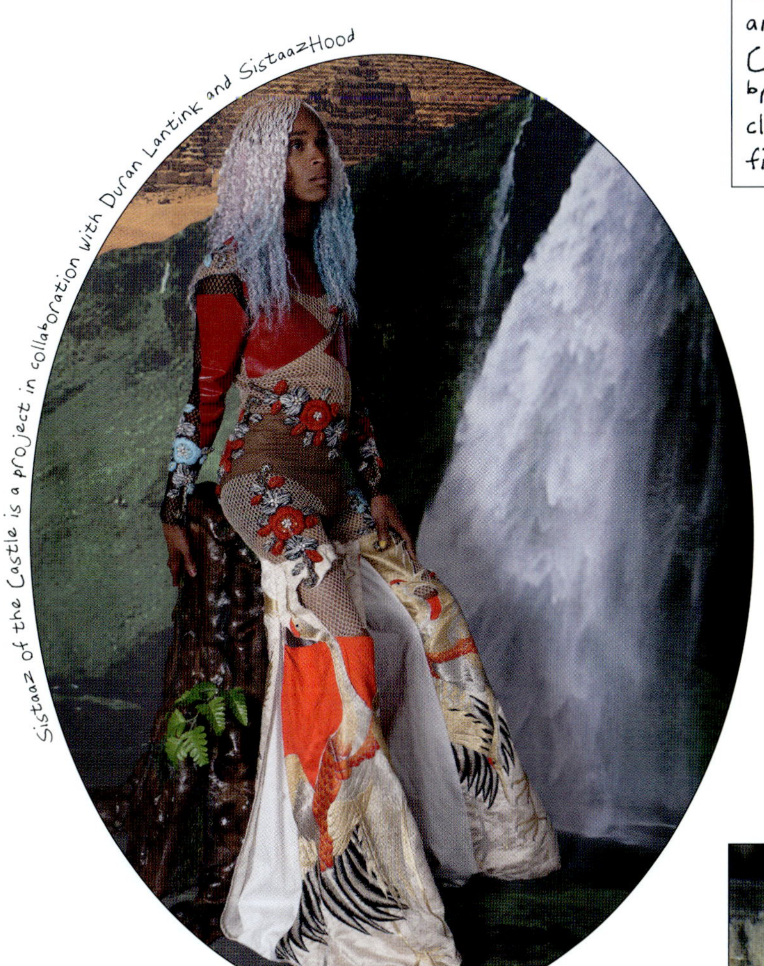
Sistaaz of the Castle is a project in collaboration with Duran Lantink and SistaazHood

and trans sex workers in Cape Town who live under a bridge but make their own clothes from things they find on the street

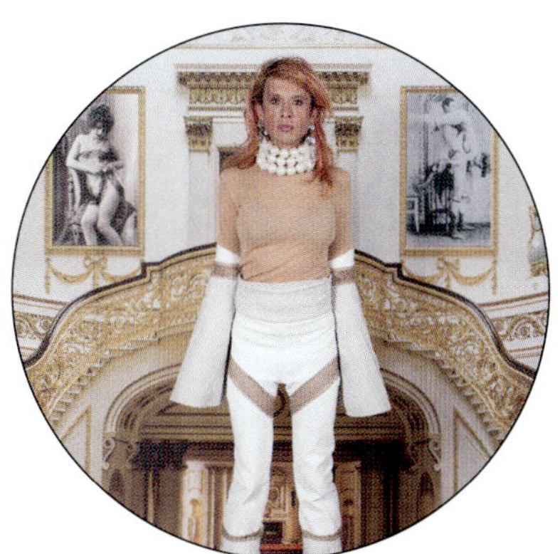

and the most colorful people I met on the street

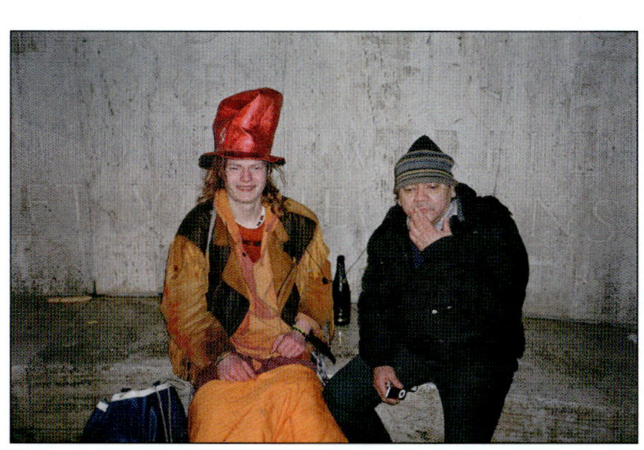

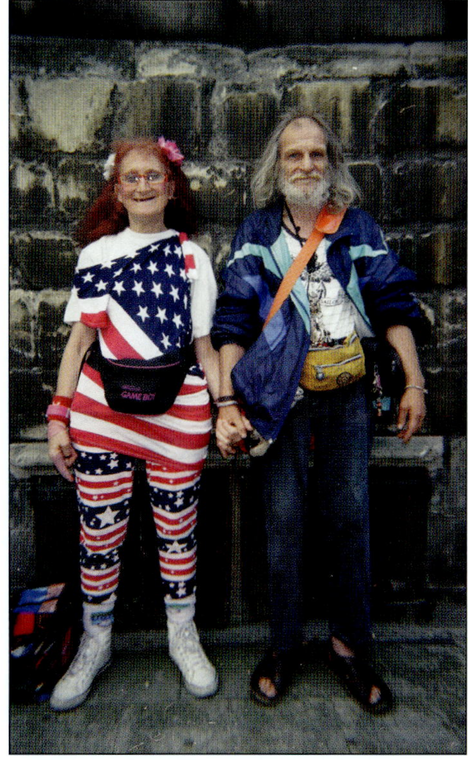

Bruin, the boy I babysit

But I don't only admire these people, all of them living in their own world, spending so little time thinking about what others think of them. I'm also jealous.

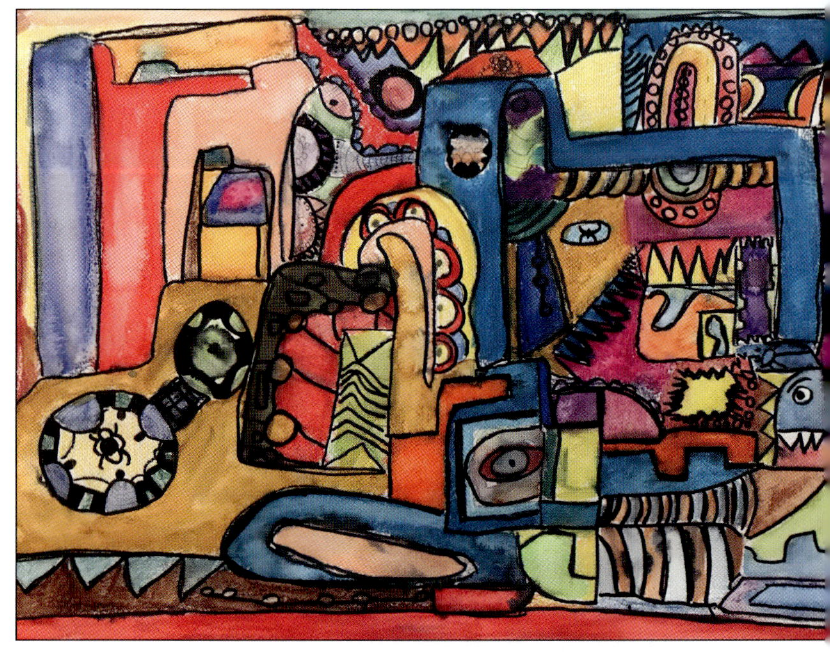

Take Bruin Parry for instance. He's a boy with Down syndrome and great artistic talent who I've been babysitting for 18 years. Once he starts drawing he seems to connect directly to this mysterious inner world, and out comes all of his remarkable brilliance, flowing onto the paper as unique geometric shapes.

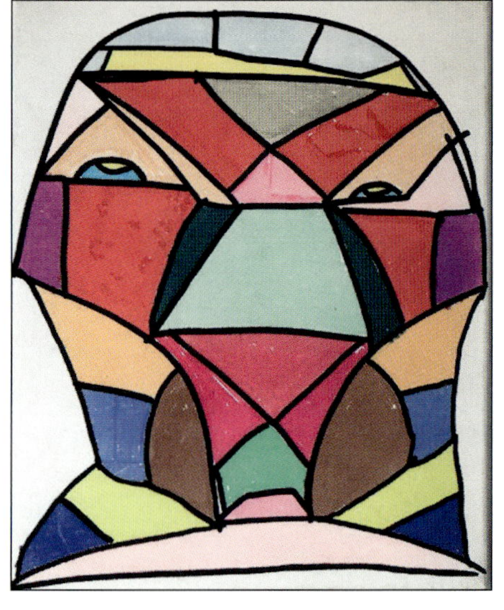

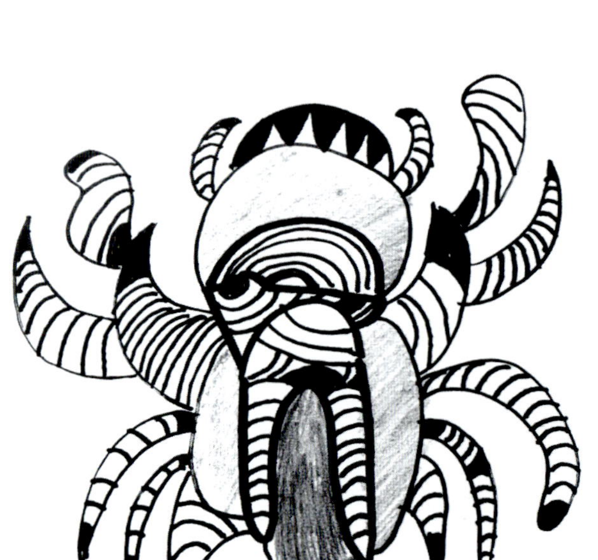

It's so different from the time I spent at the art academy. Everyone there had their own mental health issues, almost all of them either seeing a therapist or on medication, including me. And all of us fretting endlessly about what shape we should give to our "madness", with the resulting work hardly ever being as authentic as Bruin's creations.

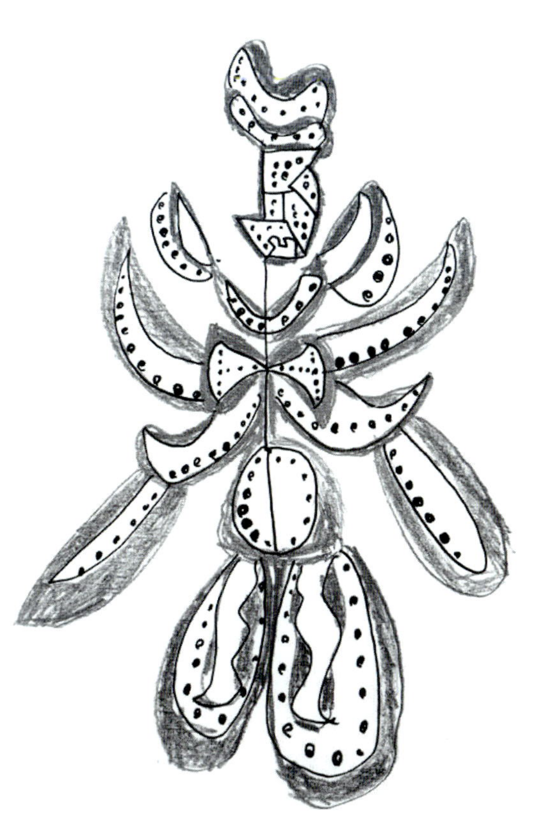

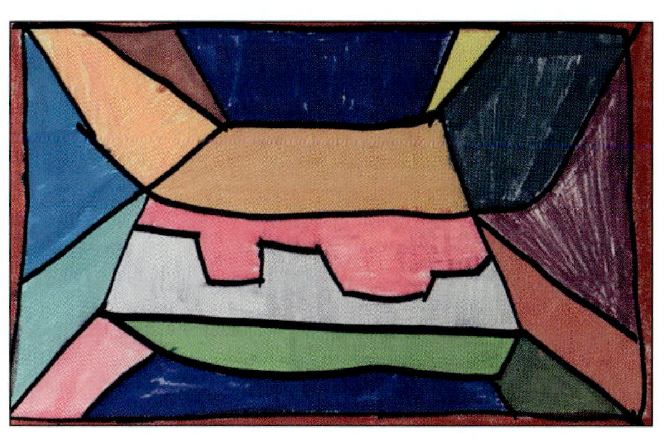

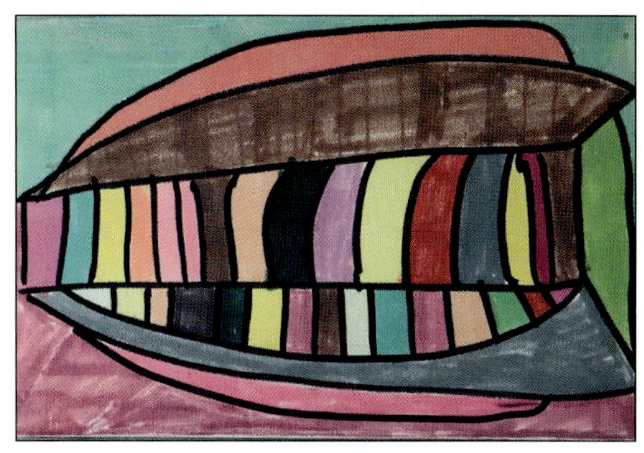

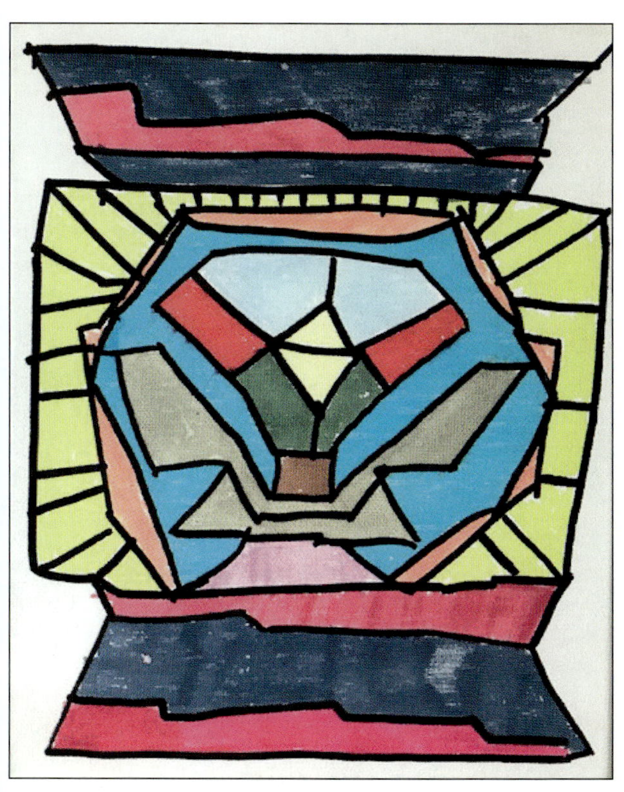

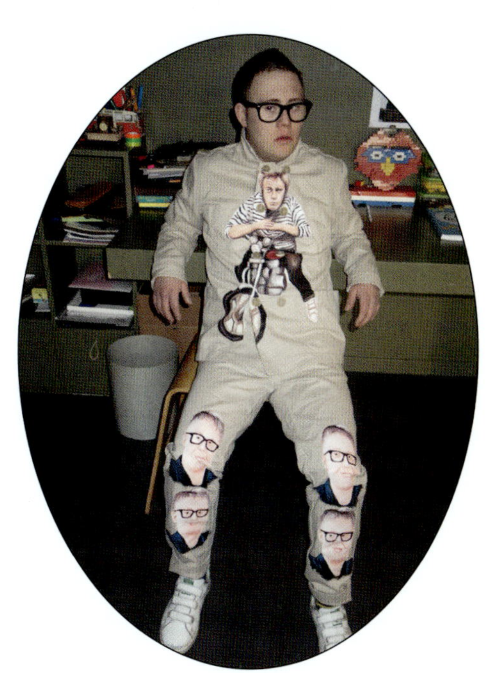

Drawings by
Bruin Parry
Insta: Bruin_parry

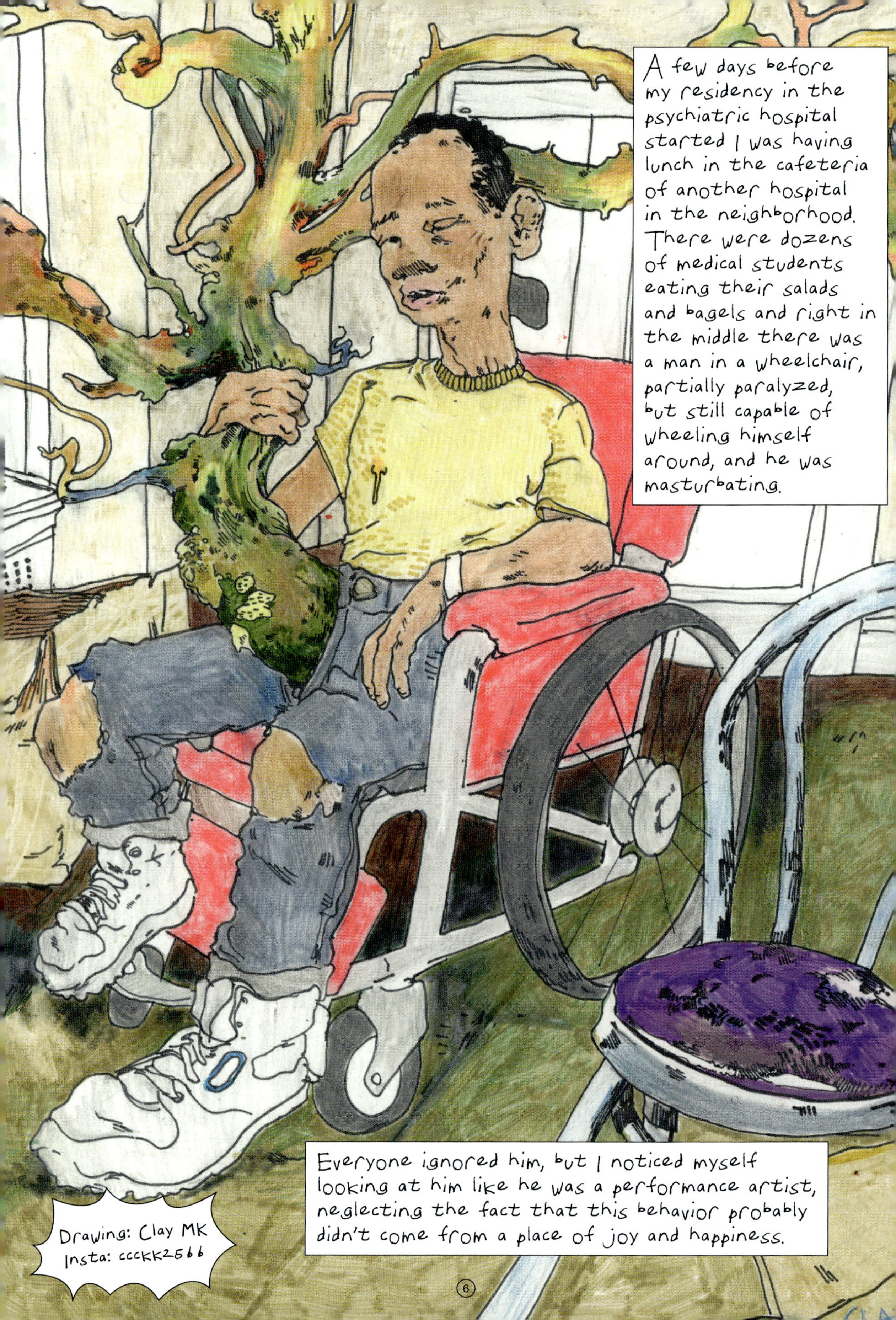
A few days before my residency in the psychiatric hospital started I was having lunch in the cafeteria of another hospital in the neighborhood. There were dozens of medical students eating their salads and bagels and right in the middle there was a man in a wheelchair, partially paralyzed, but still capable of wheeling himself around, and he was masturbating.
Everyone ignored him, but I noticed myself looking at him like he was a performance artist, neglecting the fact that this behavior probably didn't come from a place of joy and happiness.
Drawing: Clay MK
Insta: ccckk2566

The same rules don't apply to me.
When my mind fails me I tend to
sink into a tired, hazy state
I lose my feeling for language and can't speak
or write a
proper sentence.
I become too weary to even make art.
I find there is nothing to romanticize about
my own craziness.

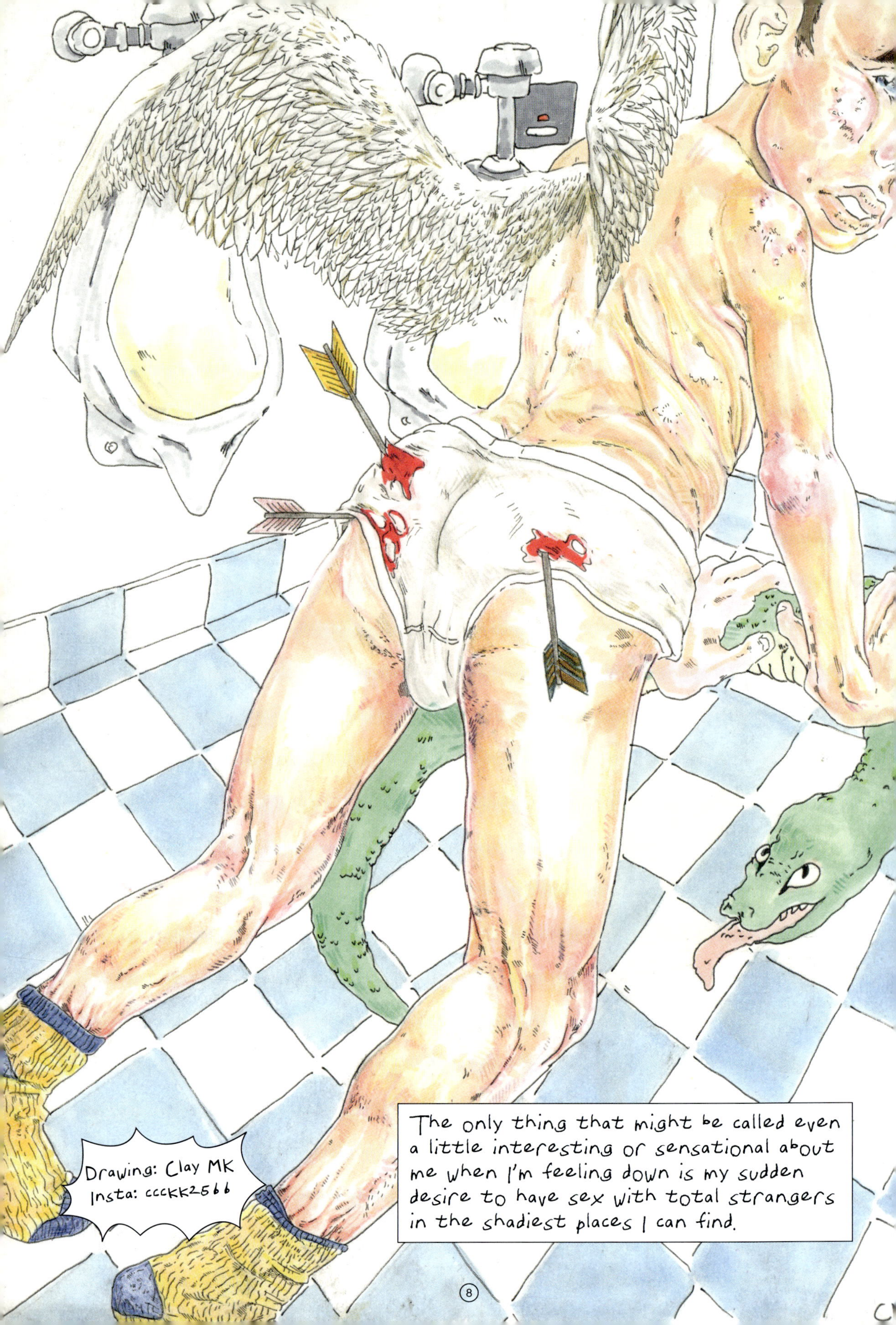
Drawing: Clay MK
Insta: ccckk2566
The only thing that might be called even a little interesting or sensational about me when I'm feeling down is my sudden desire to have sex with total strangers in the shadiest places I can find.

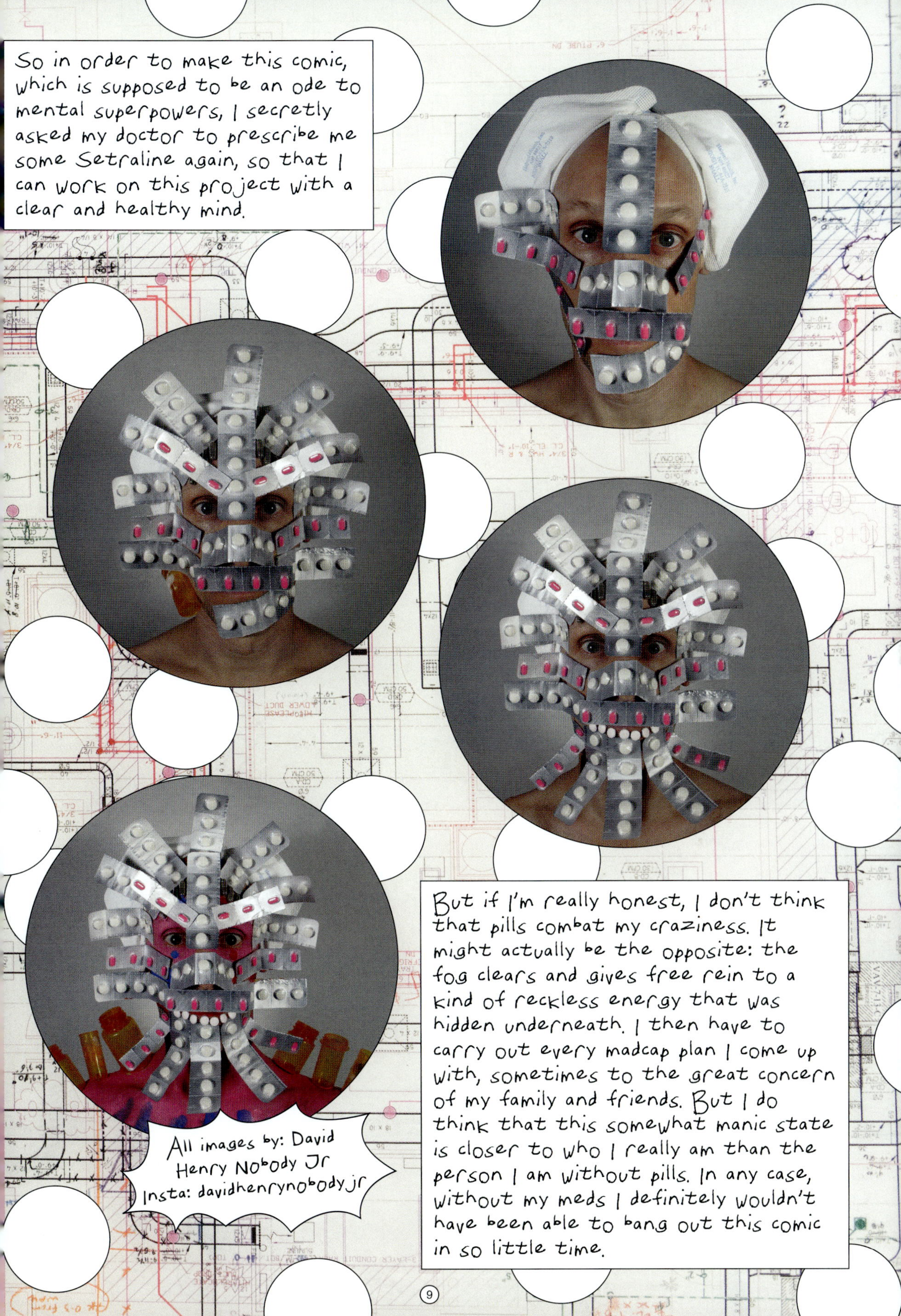
So in order to make this comic, which is supposed to be an ode to mental superpowers, I secretly asked my doctor to prescribe me some Setraline again, so that I can work on this project with a clear and healthy mind.
But if I'm really honest, I don't think that pills combat my craziness. It might actually be the opposite: the fog clears and gives free rein to a kind of reckless energy that was hidden underneath. I then have to carry out every madcap plan I come up with, sometimes to the great concern of my family and friends. But I do think that this somewhat manic state is closer to who I really am than the person I am without pills. In any case, without my meds I definitely wouldn't have been able to bang out this comic in so little time.
All images by: David Henry Nobody Jr
Insta: davidhenrynobodyjr

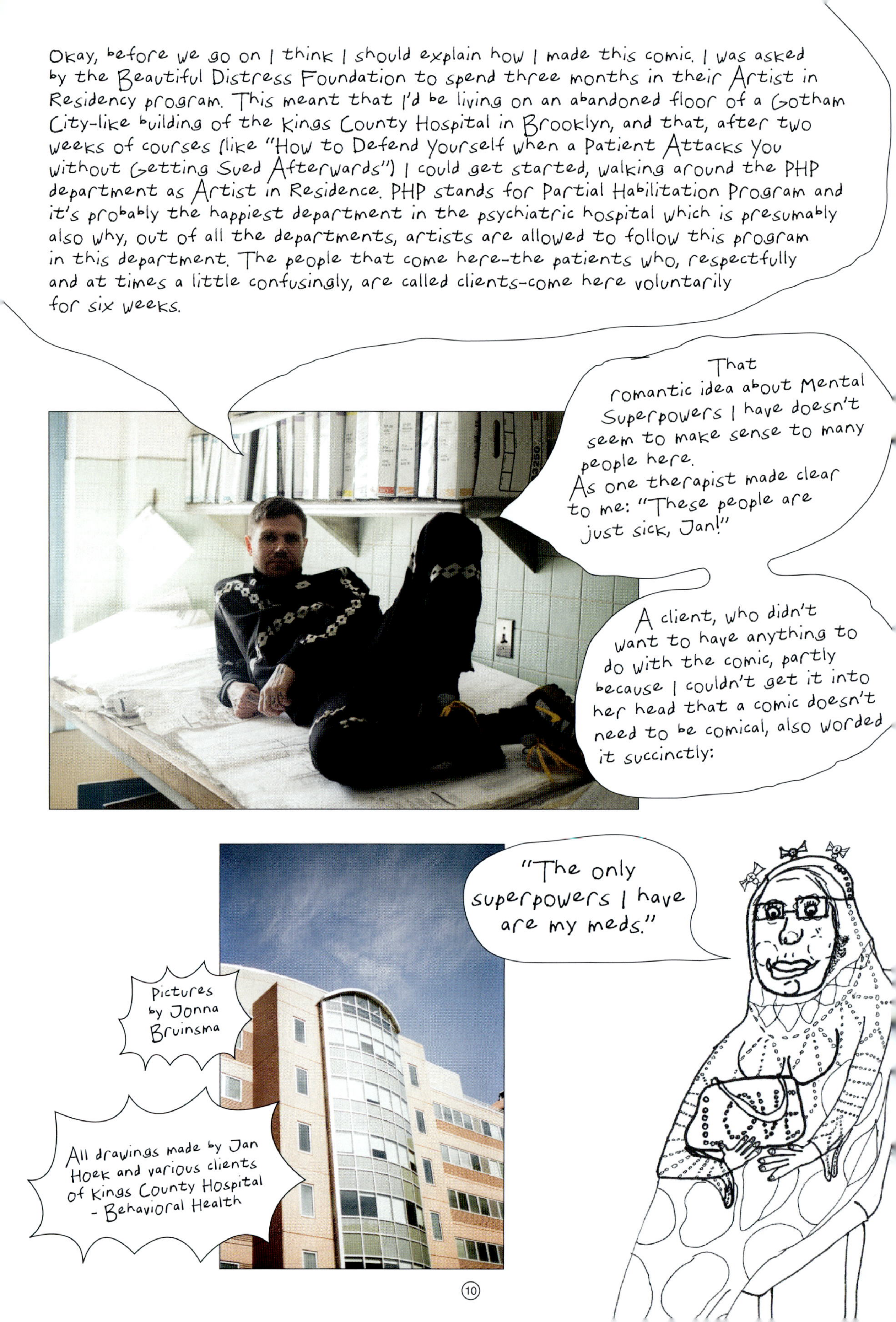

Okay, before we go on I think I should explain how I made this comic. I was asked by the Beautiful Distress Foundation to spend three months in their Artist in Residency program. This meant that I'd be living on an abandoned floor of a Gotham City-like building of the Kings County Hospital in Brooklyn, and that, after two weeks of courses (like "How to Defend yourself when a Patient Attacks You without Getting Sued Afterwards") I could get started, walking around the PHP department as Artist in Residence. PHP stands for Partial Habilitation Program and it's probably the happiest department in the psychiatric hospital which is presumably also why, out of all the departments, artists are allowed to follow this program in this department. The people that come here-the patients who, respectfully and at times a little confusingly, are called clients-come here voluntarily for six weeks.

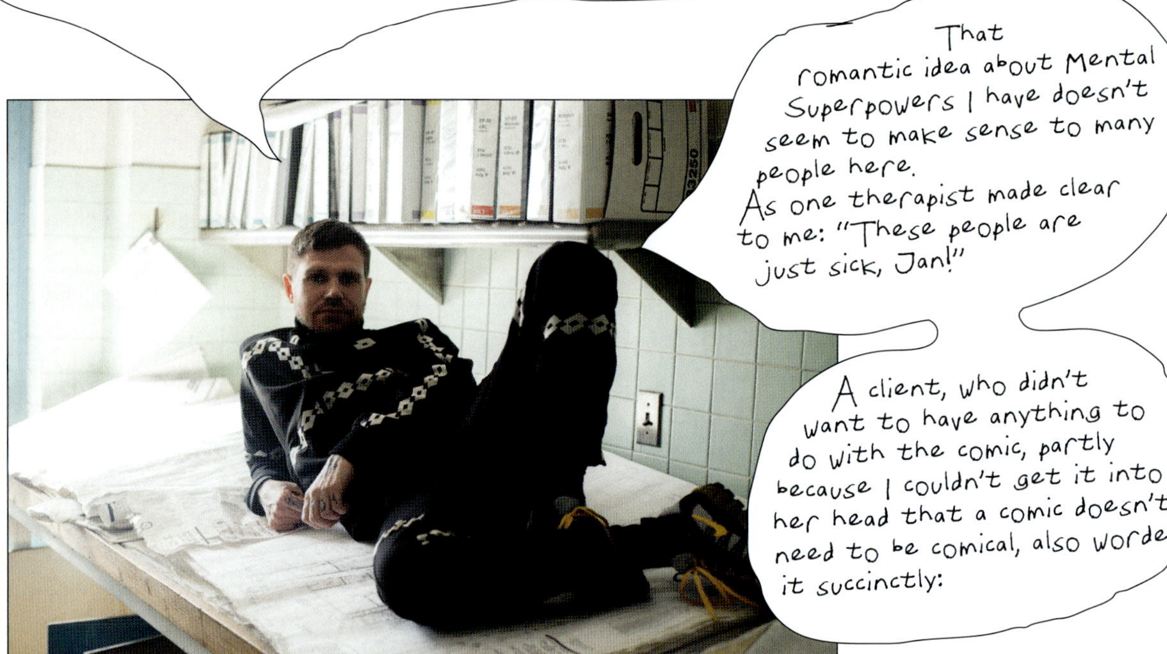

"The only superpowers I have are my meds."

Pictures by Jonna Bruinsma

All drawings made by Jan Hoek and various clients of Kings County Hospital - Behavioral Health

But at the same time, I did meet them; those clients with a brain so unique they can barely function in the normal world. Of course, they weren't following the program without a reason either, but at the same time, they were capable of the most unique, original and often intelligent mental leaps. And it was striking too, I have to say, how many writers, artists and other creative minds there were among the clients. Some had only discovered their talent in the hospital, others had, like me, made it into their profession, and it was only because of the context of this hospital that they were the patients and I wasn't.

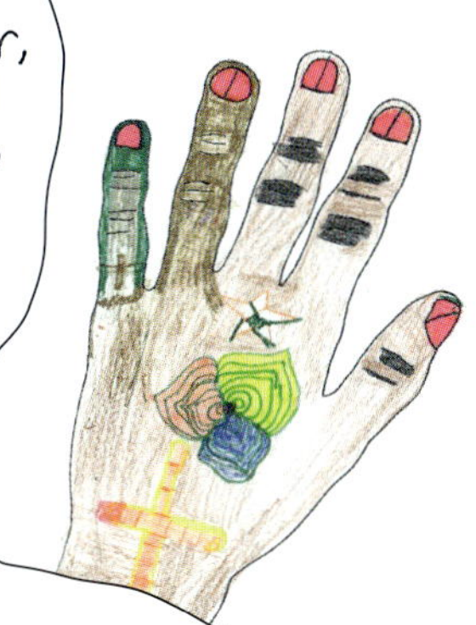

The difference between me and "them" was pretty diffuse, anyway. It took most of the staff members a few days to discover I wasn't a patient, despite my hospital badge saying "Artist in Residence". Some patients didn't realize at all. Like a surprising number of patients, I had tattoos on my hands and it was just as nice for me to be able to talk about my fears in group therapy.

While I was in New York I also reached out to a number of artists, photographers and stylists I admire. Some, "the coolest kid in class" type, I knew from Instagram and were still very young. Others were a bit more established, though I'm never that interested in the really established names. In art too, I like the outsiders the most.

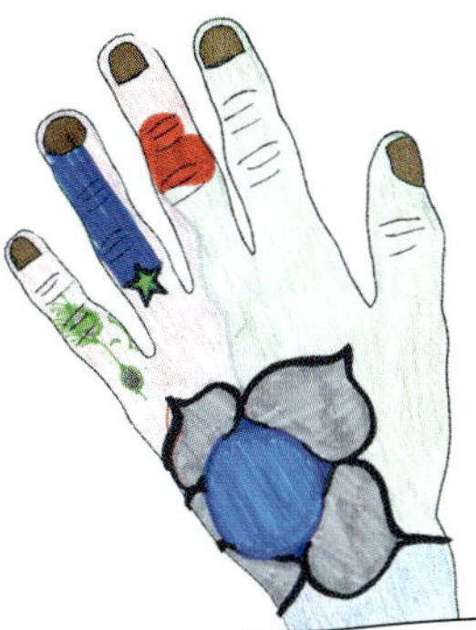

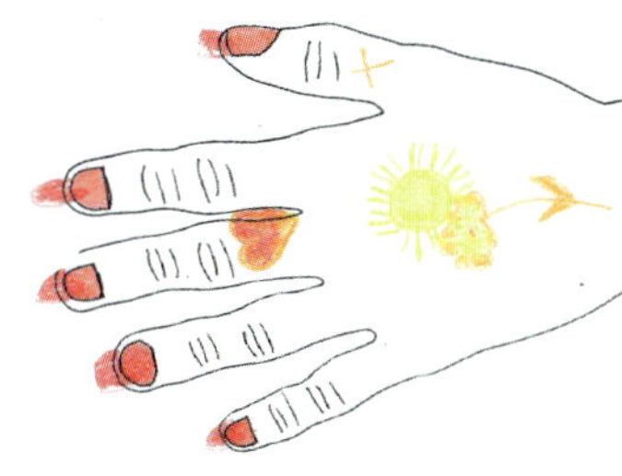

I don't know if it's some miraculous coincidence, but almost all of these artists and creators I met told me stories about themselves which were perfectly similar to those of the clients in the hospital. Even the guy I dated in New York turned out to be an artist and suffered from deep depression and anxiety every now and then. It might be because my own antidepressants were doing their job that I saw a positive side to all of this, but I thought this overlap was beautiful, as if we were all one big family. And I tried to compose this comic in that spirit. The entries by patients and by artists outside of the hospital are all in no particular order because, really, what's the difference?

Some patients immediately understood what the theme meant to me and wanted to join in talking about it, philosophizing and critiquing it. Others just wanted to show their Mental Superpower or show that conquering a mental illness is a superpower in and of itself. Still others, wanted to contribute in a simpler way; there were for instance, clients who really enjoyed coloring, which was also fine. And I also tried to engage openly with all the artists outside of the hospital to see how they wanted their contribution to take shape. Some wanted to run with it by themselves while others wanted me to write the text for their work and came up with ideas which they wanted me to execute.

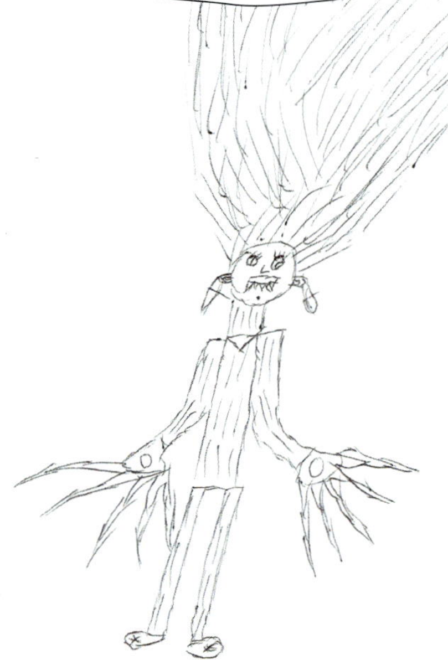

Though I have my own ideas about Mental Superpowers, which I do talk about in the comic, in the end I wanted to incorporate as many approaches, ideas and tastes as possible, from avant-garde to sappy, from technical perfection to rough, scratchy drawings, from the wholly obvious to the mysterious and obscure; All are welcome in in the Mental Superpower family.

Before I started the residency I was really trying to not make the comic too sappy and sentimental. It turns out I'm failing at that and I'm glad. If you spend enough time walking around in a psychiatric hospital you automatically end up finding the people there more important than making art which the art world sees as "real art".

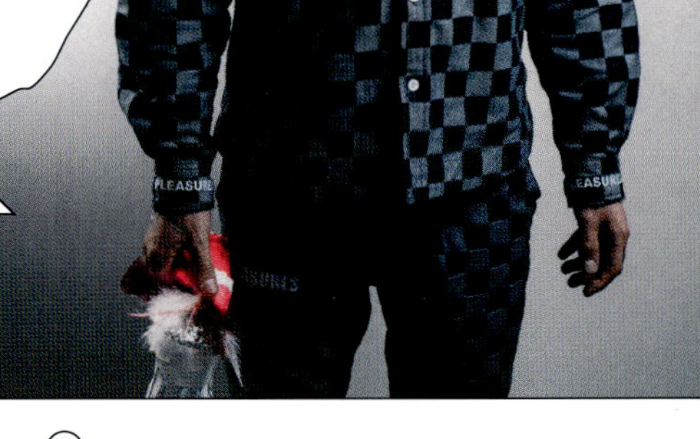

"Me as the joker during the Super Hero Fashion Show organized in the psychiatric hospital"

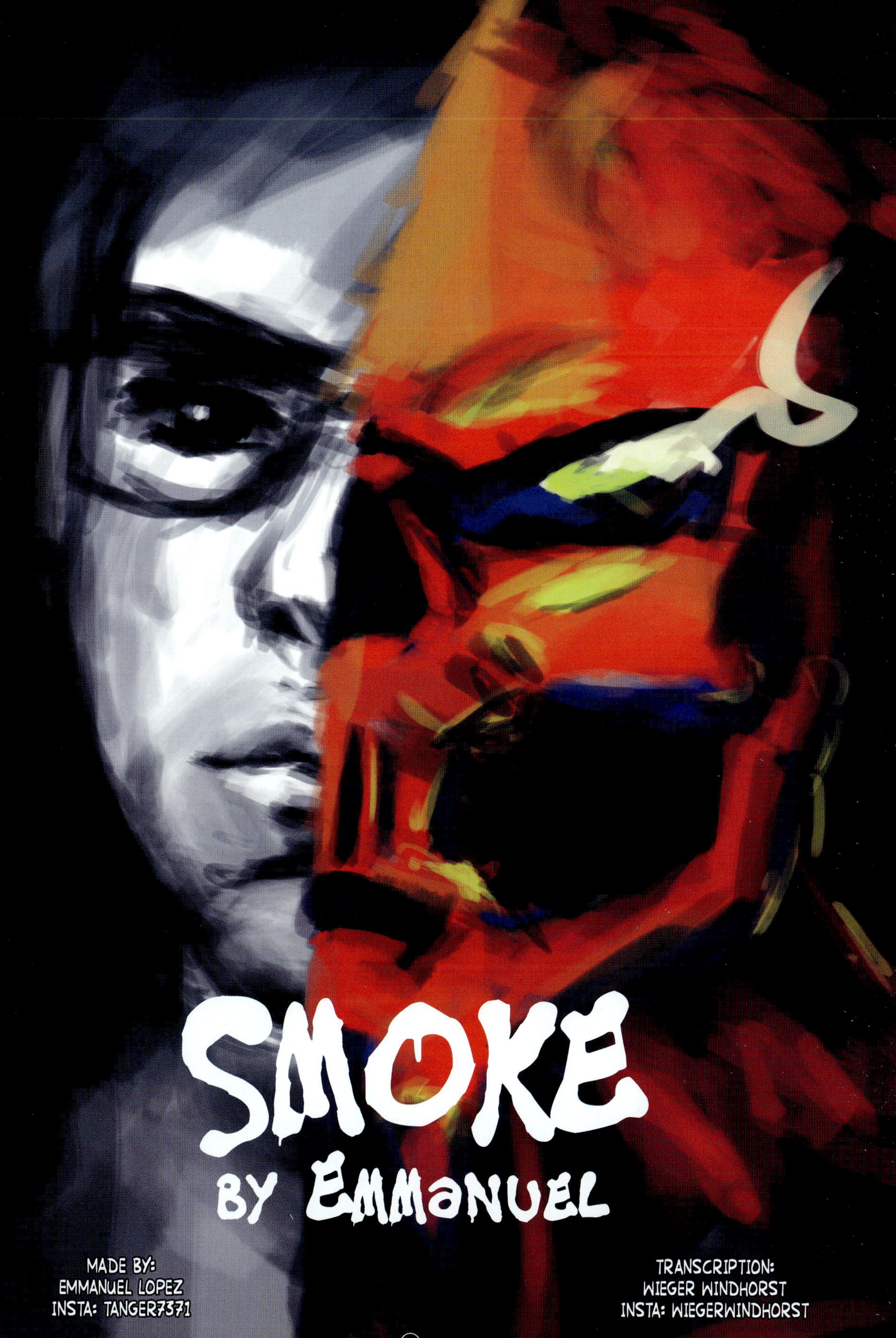
SMOKE
BY EMMANUEL
MADE BY:
EMMANUEL LOPEZ
INSTA: TANGER7371
TRANSCRIPTION:
WIEGER WINDHORST
INSTA: WIEGERWINDHORST

WELL, YOU COULD SAY THAT I'VE ALWAYS FELT THAT IT MIGHT GO WRONG ONE DAY. I MEAN, LIVING TOGETHER WITH MY GIRL IN NEW JERSEY WAS A CUSHY LIFE AND EVERYTHING, BUT MY GIRLFRIEND, I DON'T KNOW...

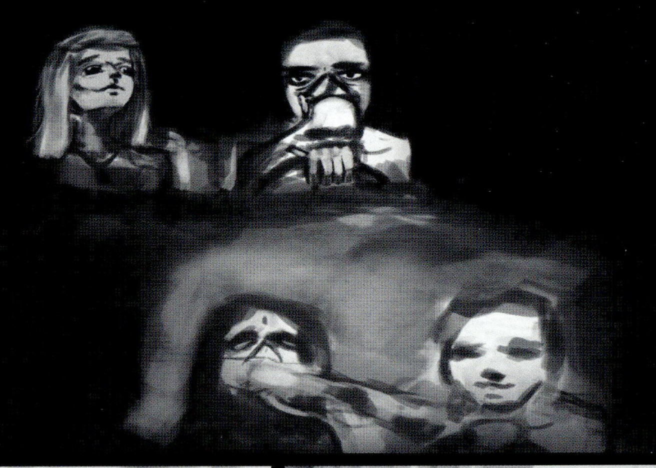

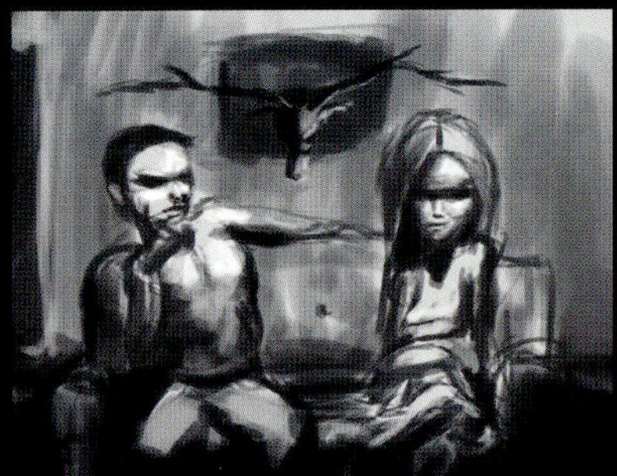

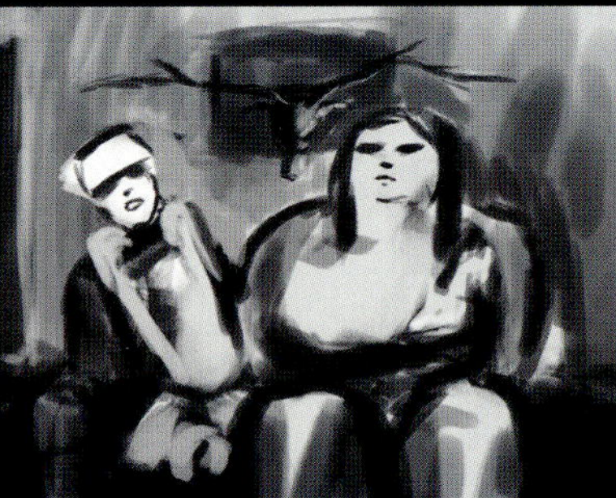

WE USED TO GET HIGH AND WATCH THE TUBE EVERY NIGHT AND EVERYTHING SEEMED JUST FINE, BUT SHE BECAME BOSSIER AND STARTED TO TAKE UP MORE SPACE.

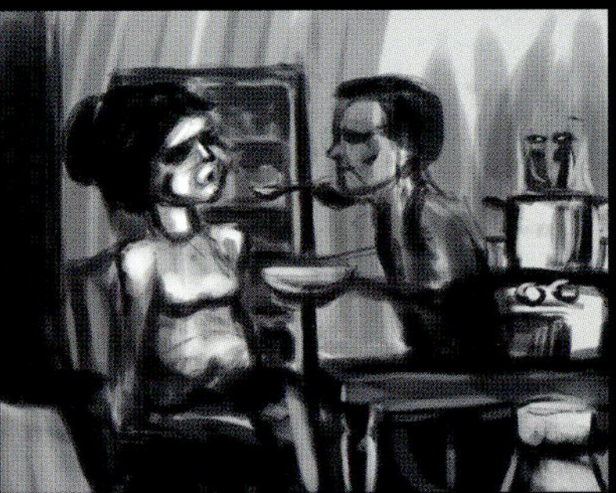

I DECIDED NOT TO WORRY ABOUT IT TOO MUCH.

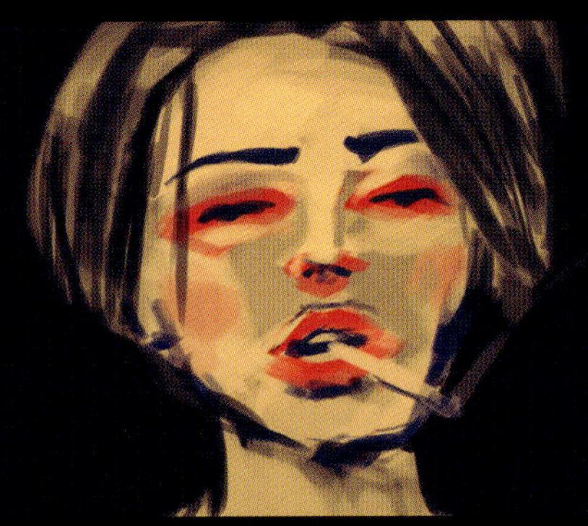

SMOKING, FOR US, WAS ALMOST LIKE WEARING A MASK; WE DIDN'T NEED TO SHOW OUR REAL SELVES...

I DON'T KNOW... THINGS JUST BECAME TOO MESSY.

SO, NOW I WAS OUT THERE ON MY OWN. I DECIDED TO GO BACK TO MY MOTHER'S HOUSE IN BROOKLYN.

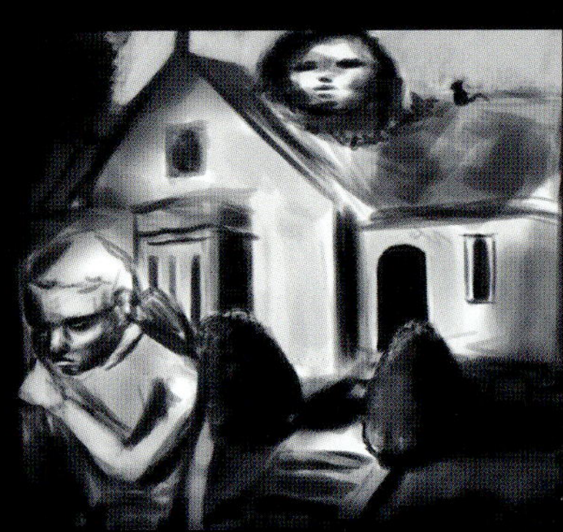

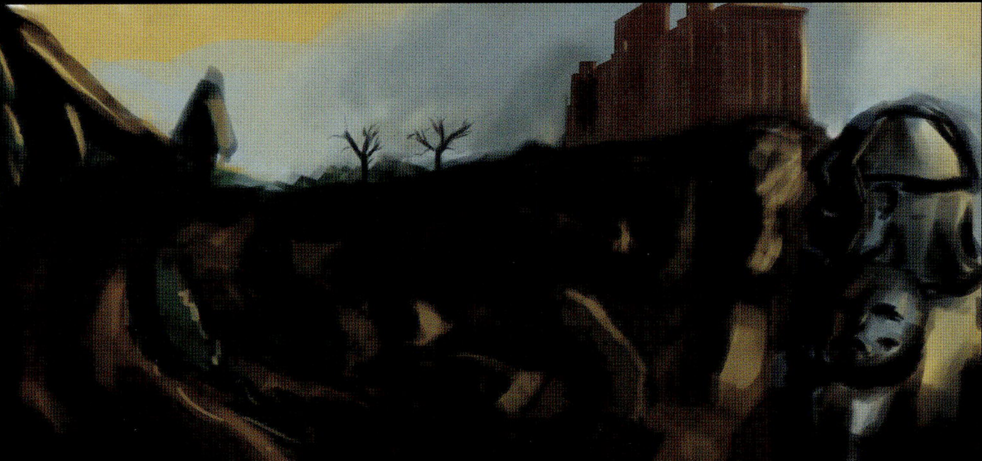

AND THAT'S WHERE I HAD TO FACE AN OLD DEMON. IT WAS STRANGE: HE CAME OUT OF NOWHERE, BUT WHEN I SAW HIM IT WAS LIKE HE HAD ALWAYS BEEN THERE...

MY FIRST REACTION WAS TO GET RID OF HIM SO I GRABBED MY MASK AND STARTED TO FIGHT HIM,

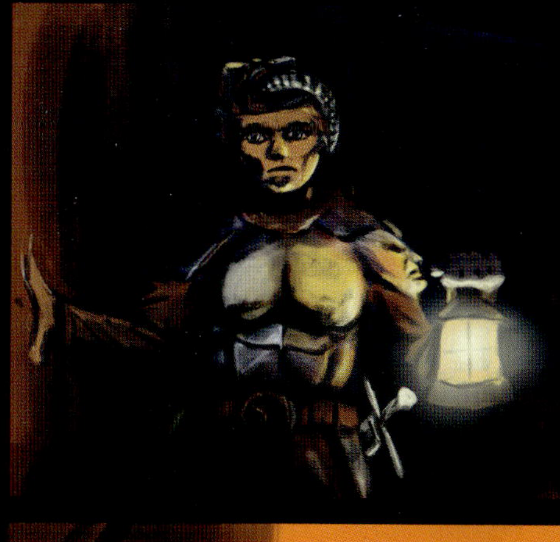

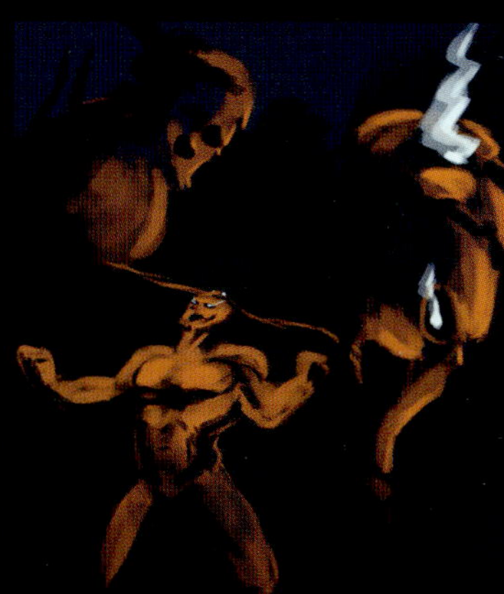

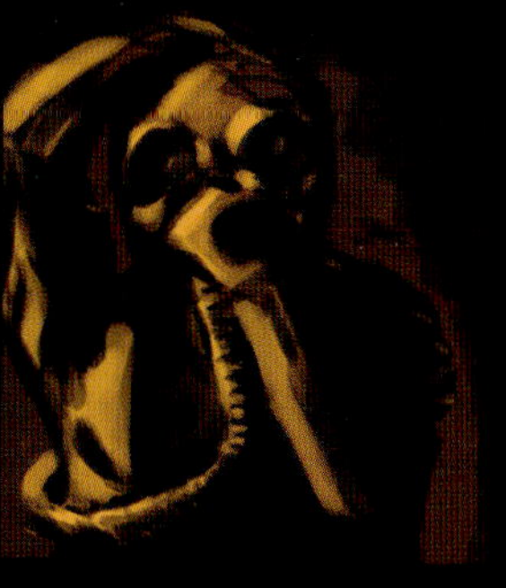

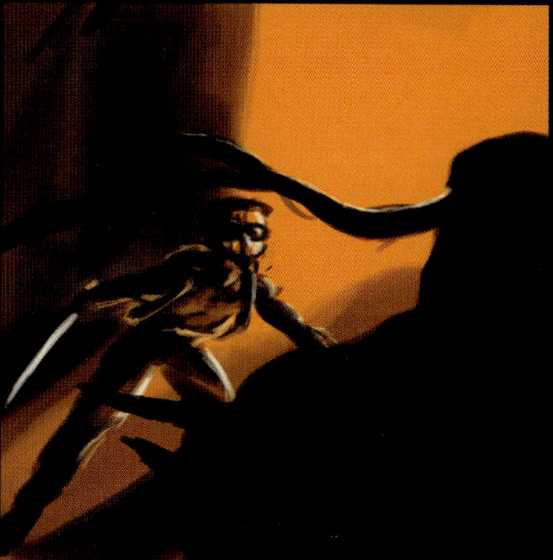

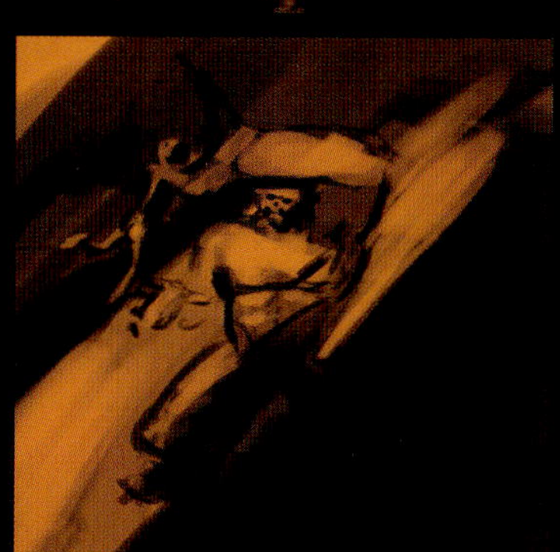

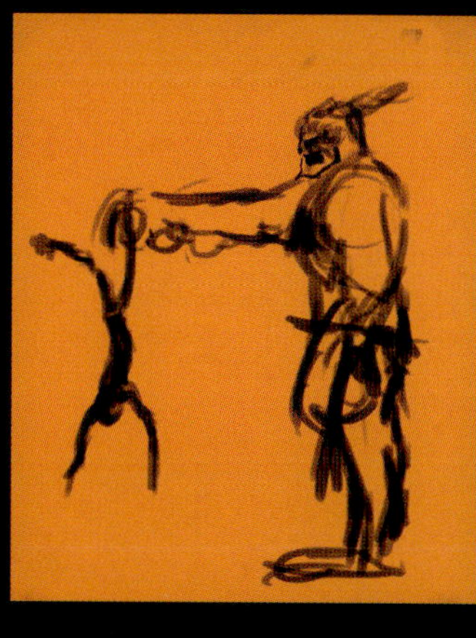

BUT I DIDN'T KNOW THAT BY FIGHTING THE DEMON, I WAS ACTUALLY FIGHTING MYSELF.

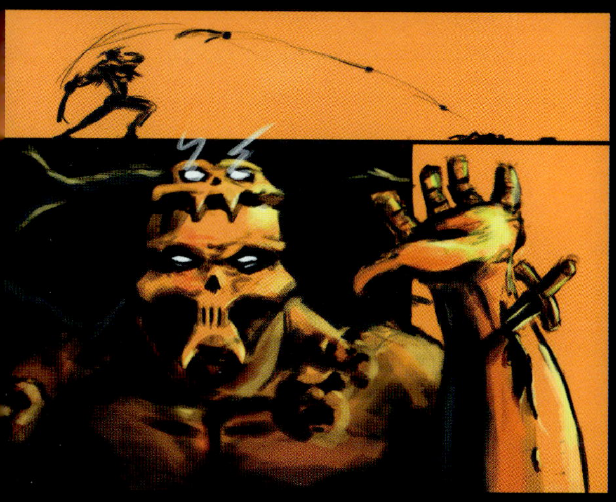

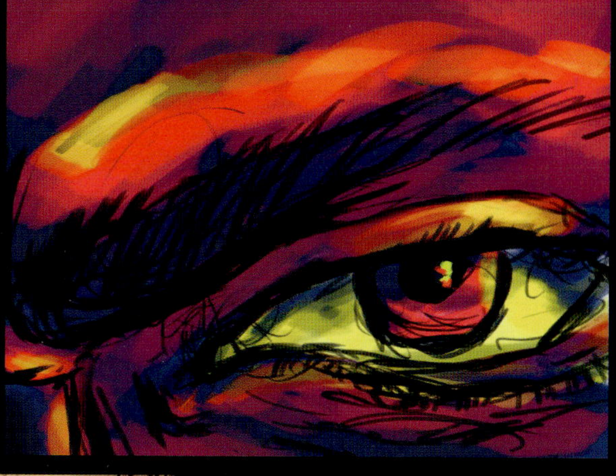

THINGS GOT A LITTLE BIT OUT OF CONTROL... AND, OH GOD, I WISH I HADN'T DONE THAT...

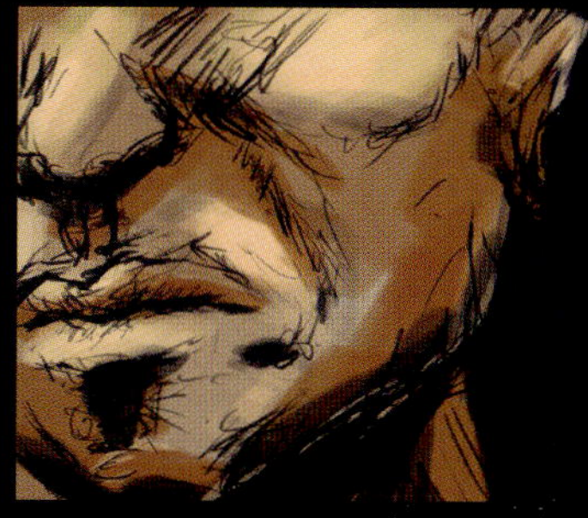

I'M NOT REALLY SURE WHAT HAPPENED NEXT. I LOST MY SENSE OF SPACE AND TIME. I JUST REMEMBER THAT I LOOKED THE DEMON RIGHT IN THE EYE AND I SAW MY OWN EYES, MY OWN FACE. IT WAS SCARY AS HELL.

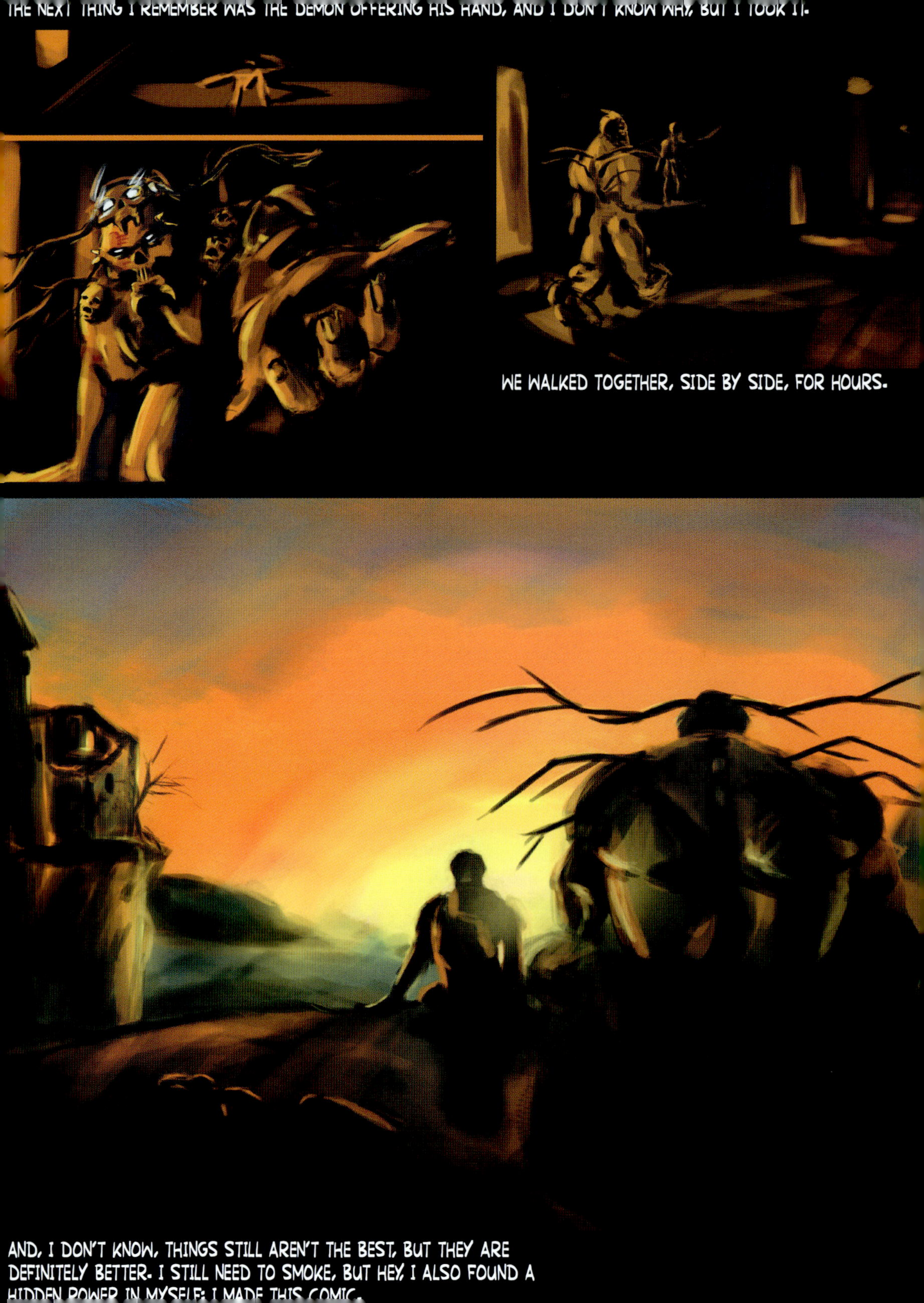

THE NEXT THING I REMEMBER WAS THE DEMON OFFERING HIS HAND, AND I DON'T KNOW WHY, BUT I TOOK IT.

WE WALKED TOGETHER, SIDE BY SIDE, FOR HOURS.

AND, I DON'T KNOW, THINGS STILL AREN'T THE BEST, BUT THEY ARE DEFINITELY BETTER. I STILL NEED TO SMOKE, BUT HEY, I ALSO FOUND A HIDDEN POWER IN MYSELF: I MADE THIS COMIC.

ALL-SEEING

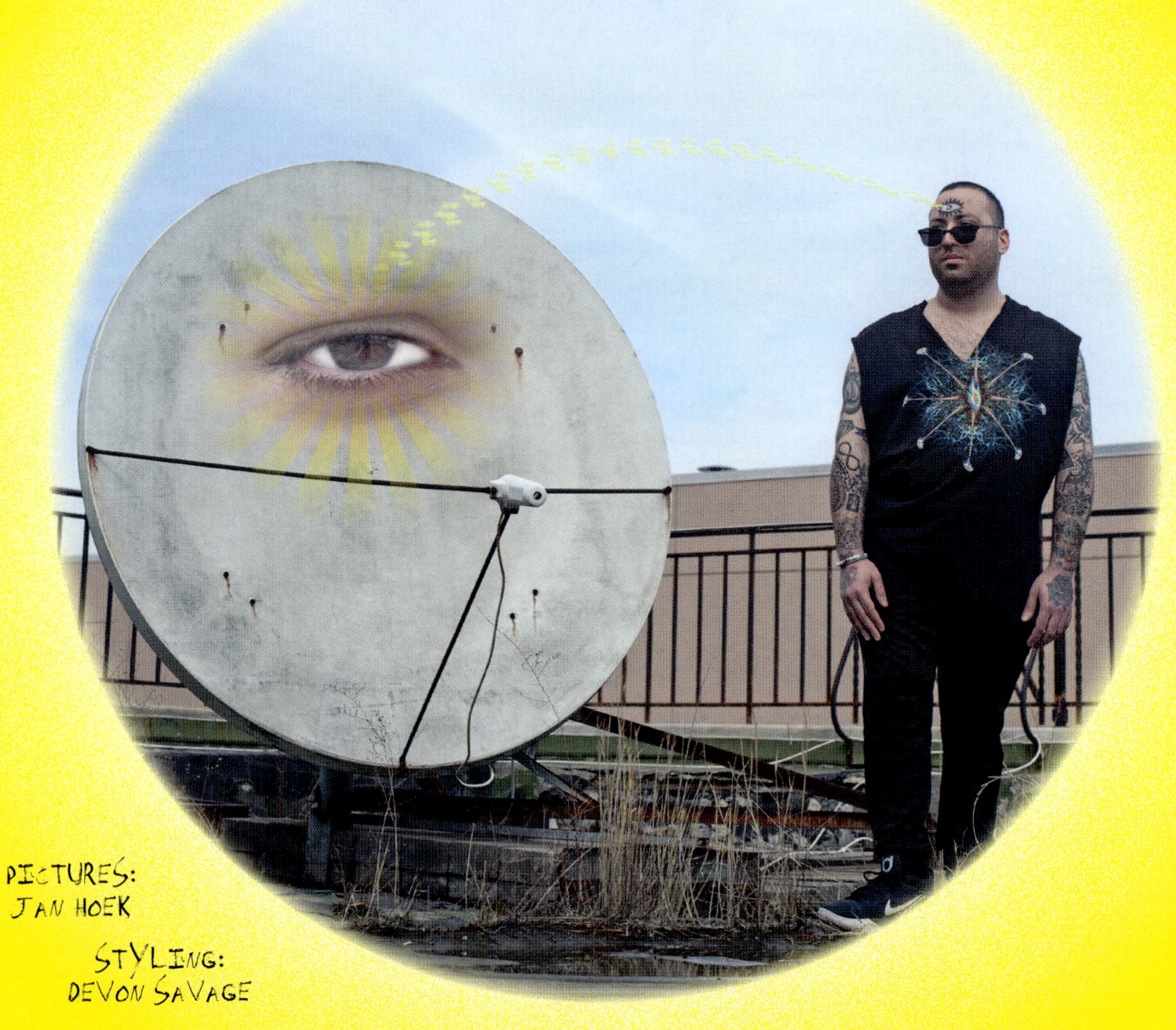

PICTURES:
JAN HOEK

STYLING:
DEVON SAVAGE

JACOB

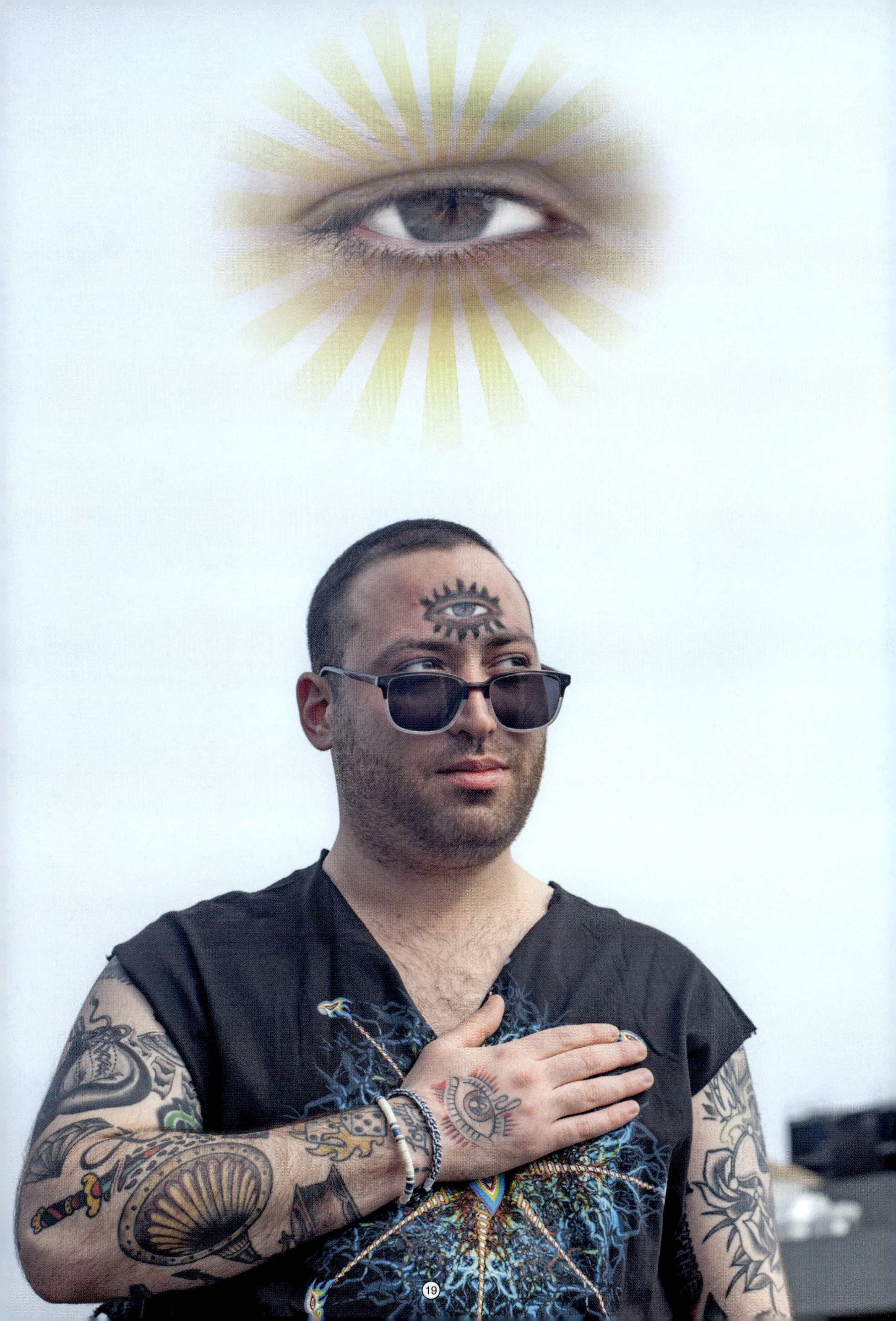

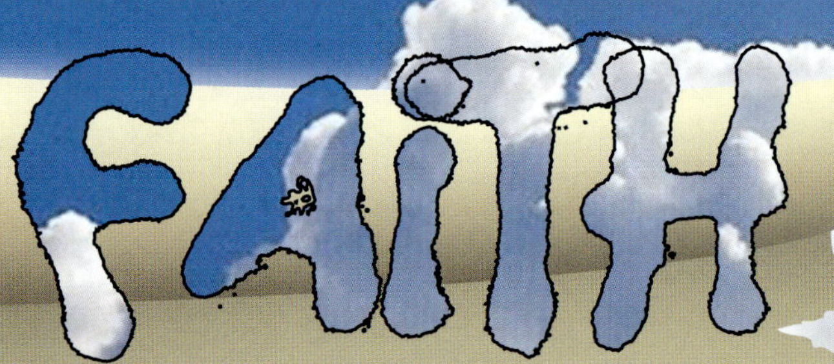

DEAR GOD,
I'M WRITING YOU THIS LETTER, EVEN THOUGH I KNOW IT'S MOSTLY FOR ME TO GET SOME THINGS OUT. LORD, I NEED YOUR HELP. I KNOW THAT YOU KNOW ALL ABOUT ME. BUT I WANT TO SHARE WITH YOU THE LITTLE THAT I THINK I KNOW ABOUT MYSELF AND I ASK YOU PLEASE TO CLEAR MY MIND, MY THOUGHTS, MY ATTITUDE OF ALL THAT IS NOT OF YOU. HERE GOES.

FATHER, YOU HAVE KEPT ME ALIVE AND WELL FOR TWENTY-EIGHT YEARS SO FAR AND FOR THAT I AM THANKFUL, BECAUSE I KNOW I WOULD NOT BE HERE RIGHT NOW WITHOUT YOU. BUT, LORD, OVER THE YEARS I MAY HAVE DONE SOME GOOD BUT I KNOW THAT I HAVE SINNED COUNTLESS TIMES. YET STILL, LORD, YOU HAVE KEPT ME. FATHER GOD, BEFORE I EVEN SAY WHAT I CAN REMEMBER, CAN YOU PLEASE FORGIVE ME AGAIN? LORD, FOR ALL THE THINGS I HAVE DONE, BOTH THOSE I WAS AWARE OF AND UNAWARE OF. GOD, I'M AT A PLACE RIGHT NOW IN MY LIFE WHERE I KNOW I NEED YOU LIKE NEVER BEFORE. STILL I FEEL AS THOUGH I'M BEING BLOCKED FROM GETTING TO YOU. LORD, IF I DON'T GET TO YOU, I WILL DIE. DYING DOESN'T SCARE ME. I'M NOT AFRAID, BUT PLEASE ALLOW ME TO GET TO KNOW YOU. FATHER, IF I RAMBLE PLEASE FORGIVE ME. IF I SIN IN ASKING ANYTHING OF YOU, PLEASE FORGIVE ME.

GOD, I'M A NEWLYWED WITH A SIX-YEAR-OLD DAUGHTER. I KNOW THAT YOU HAVE GIVEN BOTH MY HUSBAND AND MY DAUGHTER TO ME, AND YOU KNOW THAT I'M ABLE TO BE A GOOD WIFE AND MOTHER. FATHER, I NEED HELP WITH MY MARRIAGE. THERE'S NOTHING WRONG, I JUST KNOW THAT I CAN DO BETTER AND BE BETTER IF YOU HELP ME. LORD, I HAVE A DREAM AND I WANT TO SHARE THAT WITH YOU. FATHER, YOU KNOW THAT OVER THE YEARS I HAVE BEEN MOLESTED AND FORCED UPON. I HAVE HAD ABORTIONS. I HAVE FELT ALONE, SUICIDAL, NAKED, CONFUSED, AND LOST FOR YEARS. LORD, I HAVE HAD LITTLE SELF-ESTEEM AND VERY LITTLE INSPIRATION ABOUT MUCH OF ANYTHING. LORD, IN SPITE OF IT ALL, I KNOW THAT AS MUCH AS IT HURT YOU TO SEE ME ALLOW MY MIND AND BODY TO BE USED FOR EVIL, YOU, ALMIGHTY GOD, THROUGH YOUR SON, JESUS CHRIST, LOVED ME, STOOD BY ME, WATCHED OVER ME, SPOKE TO ME, PRAYED FOR ME, DIED FOR ME, ROSE FOR ME, AND WILL COME AGAIN FOR ME.

LORD, THROUGH IT ALL YOU HAVE BEEN AWESOME, MAGNIFICENT, GLORIOUS, WONDERFUL, AND EVERLASTING. LORD, YOU HAVE BEEN EVERYTHING FOR ME. EVEN WHEN I WASN'T THINKING ABOUT YOU, YOU LOVED ME.

TEXT BY:
LESLENE
O'MEALLY-WHYTE

PICTURE: JAN HOEK

PHOTOGRAPHY ASSISTANT:
SOPHIE SCHWARTS

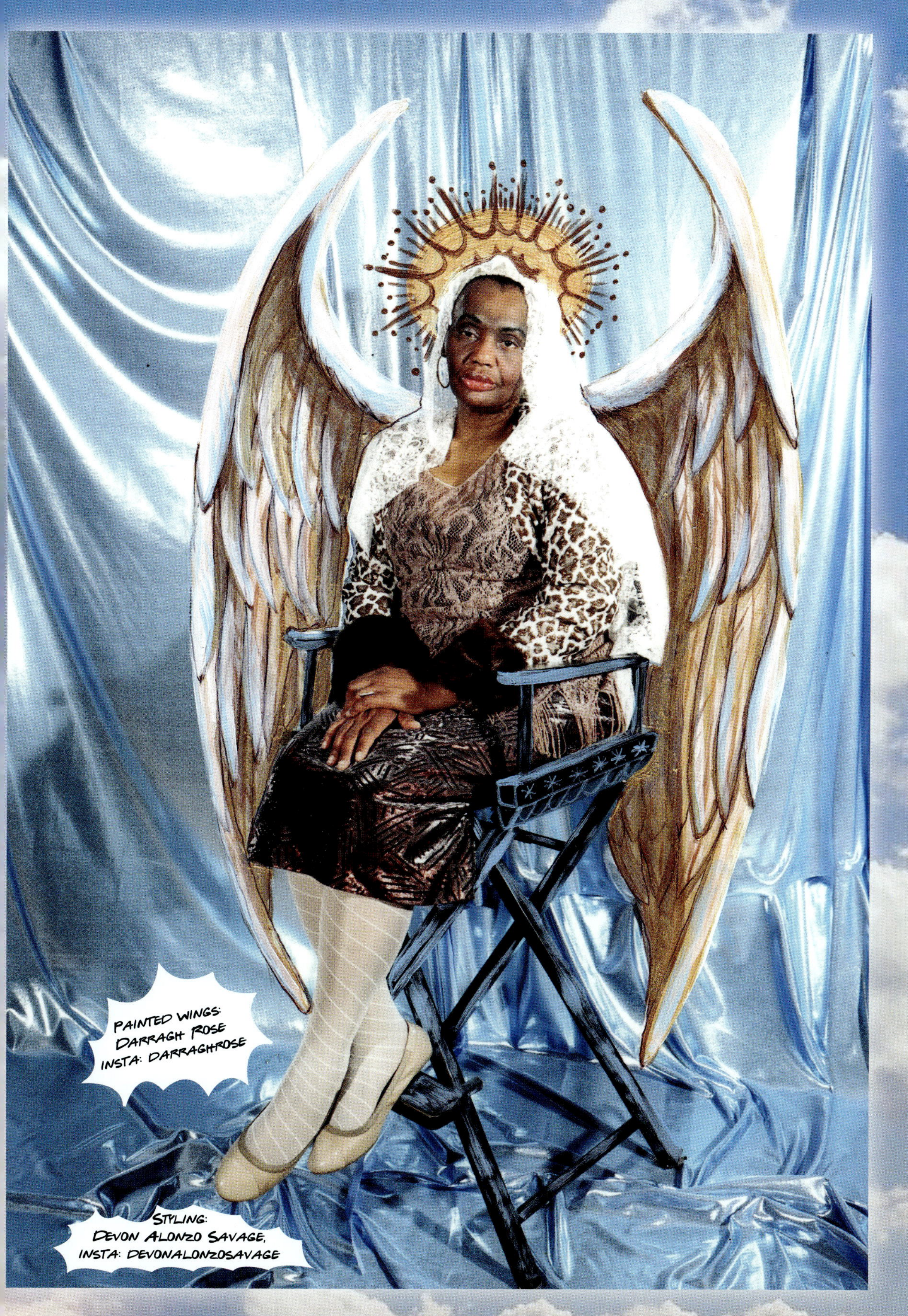
PAINTED WINGS:
DARRAGH ROSE
INSTA: DARRAGHROSE
STYLING:
DEVON ALONZO SAVAGE,
INSTA: DEVONALONZOSAVAGE

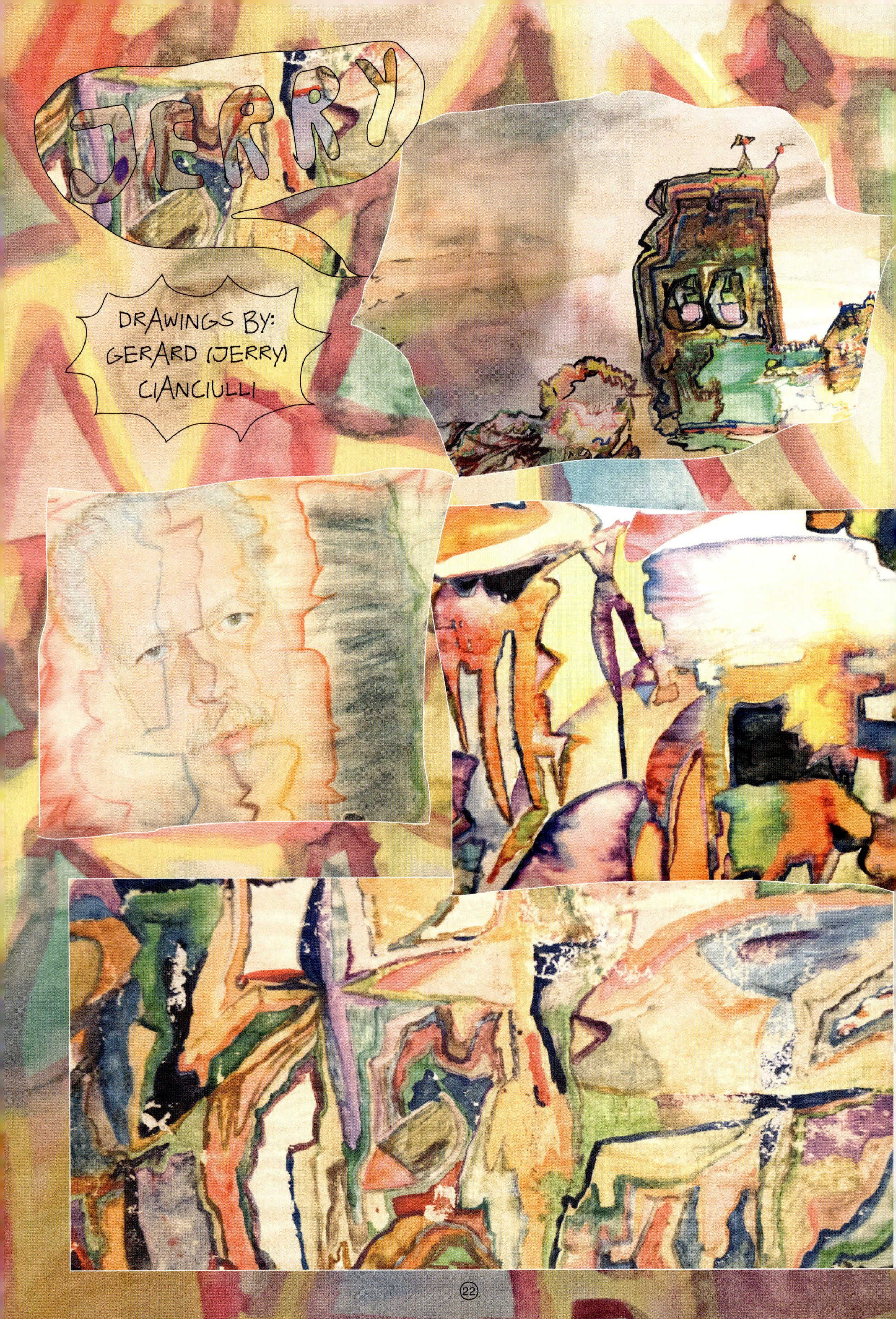
JERRY
DRAWINGS BY:
GERARD (JERRY)
CIANCIULLI

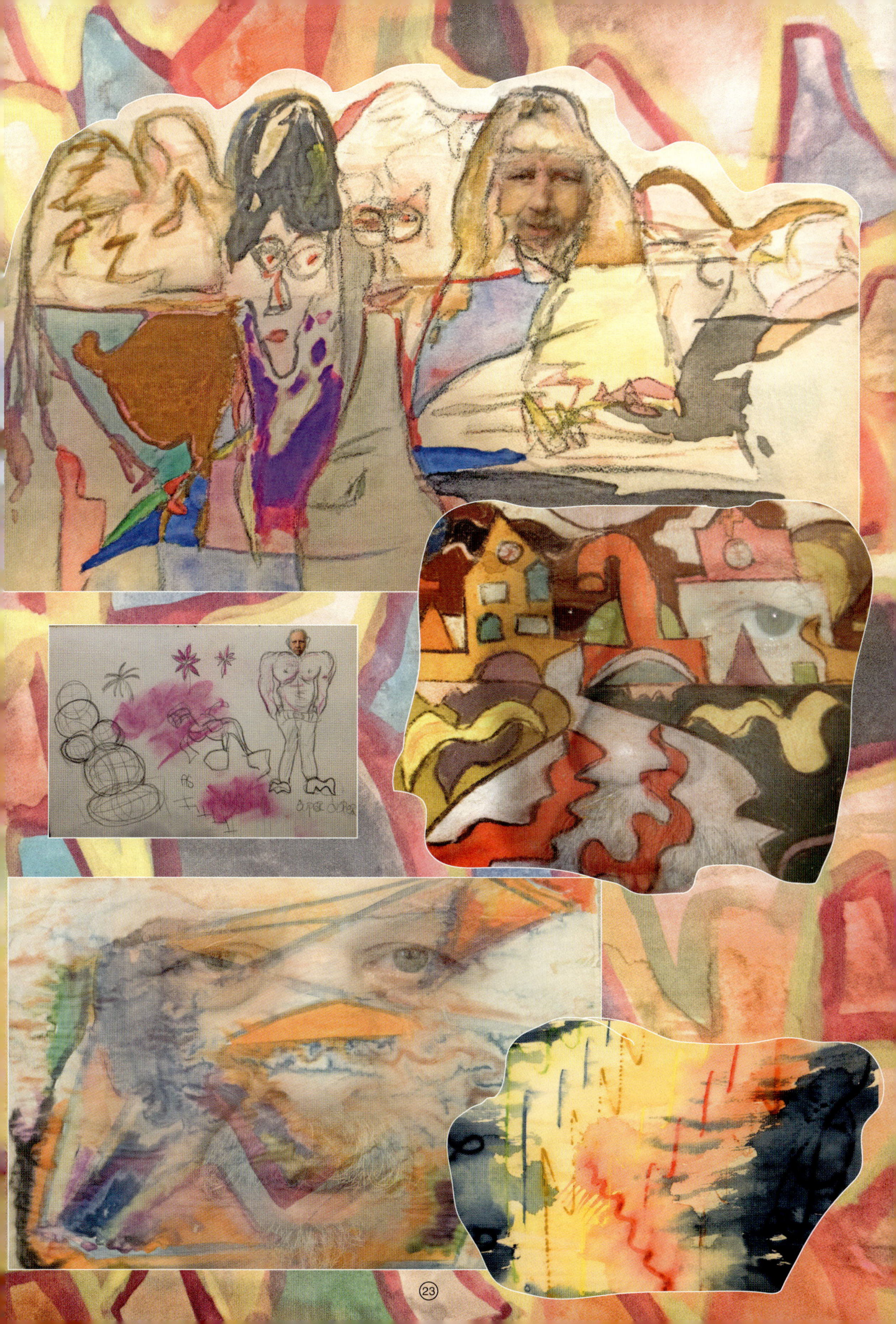

DOCTOR PRASHANT

Why did you become a psychiatrist?

I've gotten this question a thousand times, so I am aware that I've made a story of this answer that maybe transformed into a different answer from the one I would have given ten years ago, when I actually made that decision. I've always romanticized being a doctor since a young age. It brings out my personality. I'm a caring person. I love being with patients, but it wasn't the symptoms that interested me, nor the diagnosis: I'm not that doctor that cares to solve the puzzle. I was moved by people who are suffering, and I chose to become a psychiatrist because, as a psychiatrist, you work with patients who are more in touch with their suffering.

Jan Hoek by Rebertha Moore

Do you think that mental illness or wiring in your head that's different can contribute to creativity?

In the psychiatric world this is a very well-known debate. I don't think it's a precondition for being a genius. My personal thinking is that it's a way of romanticizing mental illness. I think that for every brilliant creator who is mentally ill, there are nine brilliant people who are not.

Also, then, it's interesting to think about what is mental illness and what is not. We've started to pathologize behavior much more in recent history. Only a hundred years ago you really had to smear yourself with feces before you got the label crazy. Now people who are grieving because they lost somebody they loved can already get labeled as mental.

And how your behavior is seen also depends on who you are. For example, when you're a creative artist, people tolerate more craziness from you. Let's take all the tattoos you have: because you are here as an artist, people will think "Oooh interesting, it's probably a creative expression in line with his work." When a patient comes in with the same tattoos it would be pathologized more.

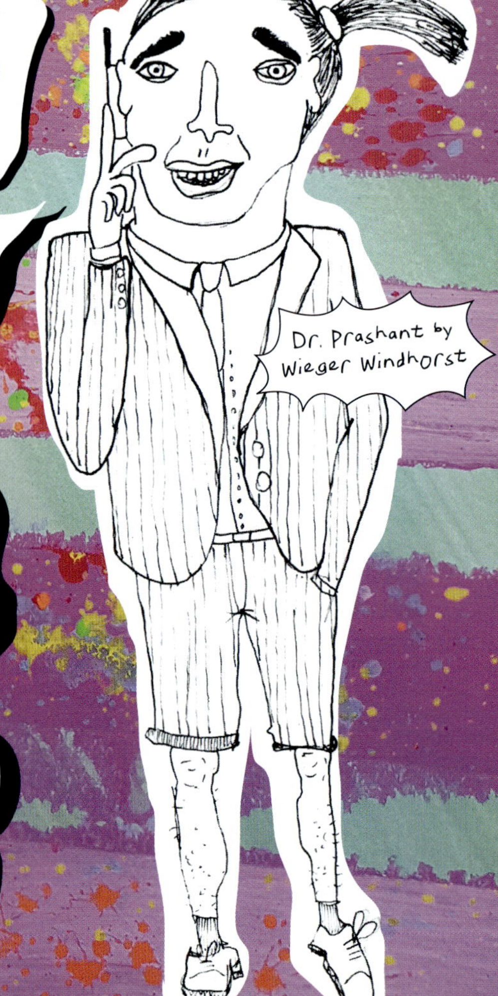

Dr. Prashant by Wieger Windhorst

Do you have the feeling that by treating or medicating patients in order to make them function again, or happy, you also take away some of their uniqueness?

I personally do feel that by medicating, they lose a bit of their own factor, that they do lose their uniqueness. Medication is a form of control; you don't cure somebody with it.

For example, there was this one patient, who was incredibly intelligent and creative. He designed fashion and had the most out of the box mythological theories about everything. When he left Kings County he was completely in his shell, almost not talking anymore, not creating anymore. You and I will think that's a pity, but his family was actually quite happy: he didn't give them any trouble anymore, no aggression.

On a personal level, do you feel love for atypical, "crazy" behavior?

I'm curious about all behavior, but I don't know if I can call it love. Whatever is outside of my understanding I try to understand. It's love because I don't reject any behavior, even though there is some behavior for which it's more difficult to feel sympathy or curiosity. For example, I had, for quite some time, a client who was a child molester. But even then I need to try to understand it.

Jan Hoek by Wieger Windhorst

Dr. Prashant by Bruin Parry

What was the most beautiful expression of a differently working mind you have ever seen?

When I worked with inpatients there was a 29 year old kid who was from Ukraine; a really bright kid. He was basically a medical student, PHD drop out, intensely smart, but also suffering a lot. He was catatonic, a state in which you almost transform into a statue. He stopped talking completely. But not saying something is also communication. He was sitting in different yoga positions and he looked very much like an Indian Sadhu. He was an example of somebody who had a very academic background. It was always about being rational and expressing yourself logically, and he broke with that and chose the spiritual path. He failed to explain to his parents why he broke with them. I tried to make a connection just by sitting with him for 45 minutes, not saying anything, just being there. After a while he started to talk; he had many spiritual philosophies that were on the edge of idiocracy. Most people that would see him, half naked, not having showered for ages, would see a crazy person. But I saw somebody who wanted to say something; someone who wanted to break with the oppressive, rational world. Maybe I also felt a connection with him because I am from an Indian background, a place where the spiritual has more of a place in society.

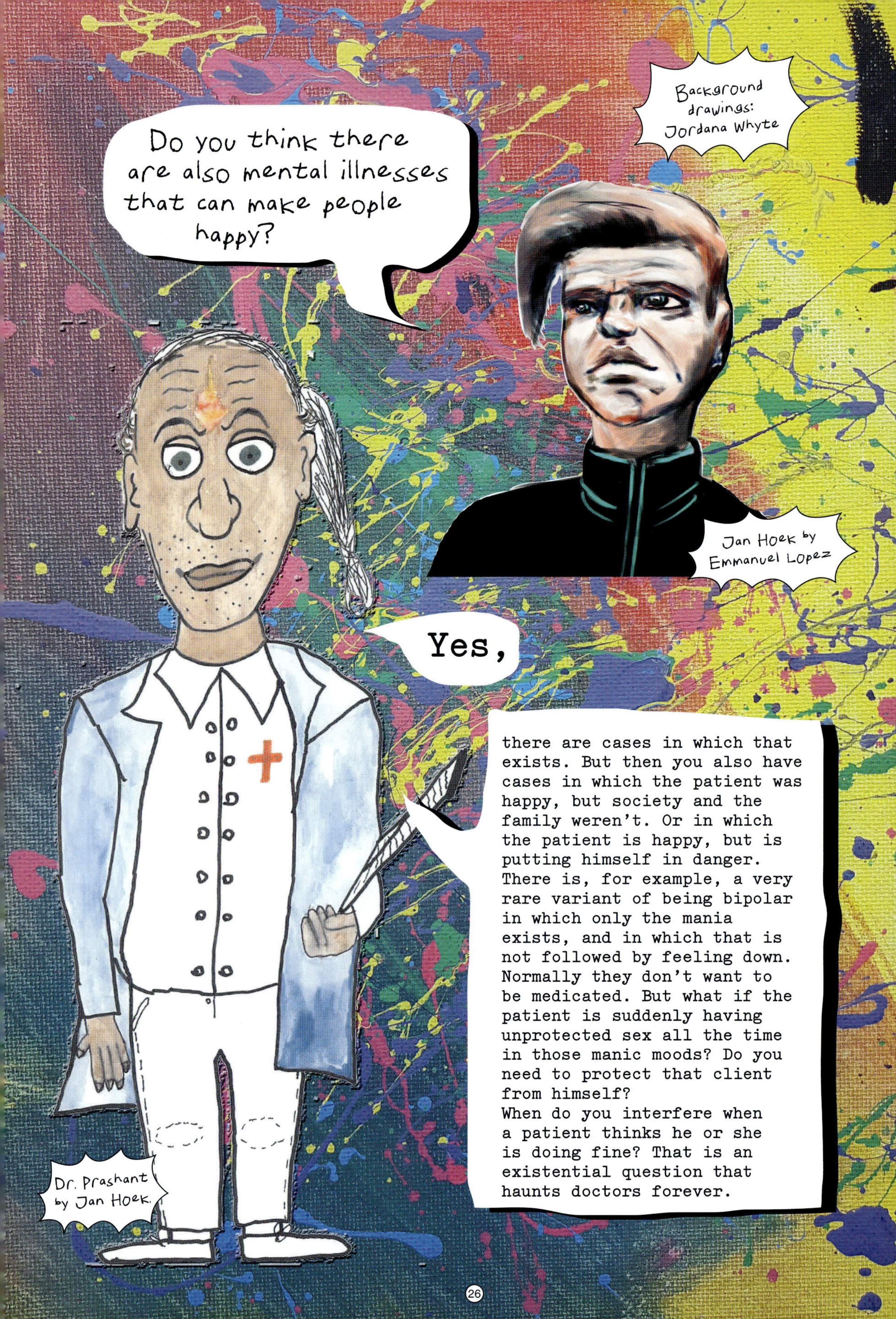
Background drawings: Jordana Whyte
Do you think there are also mental illnesses that can make people happy?
Jan Hoek by Emmanuel Lopez
Yes,
there are cases in which that exists. But then you also have cases in which the patient was happy, but society and the family weren't. Or in which the patient is happy, but is putting himself in danger. There is, for example, a very rare variant of being bipolar in which only the mania exists, and in which that is not followed by feeling down. Normally they don't want to be medicated. But what if the patient is suddenly having unprotected sex all the time in those manic moods? Do you need to protect that client from himself?
When do you interfere when a patient thinks he or she is doing fine? That is an existential question that haunts doctors forever.
Dr. Prashant by Jan Hoek.

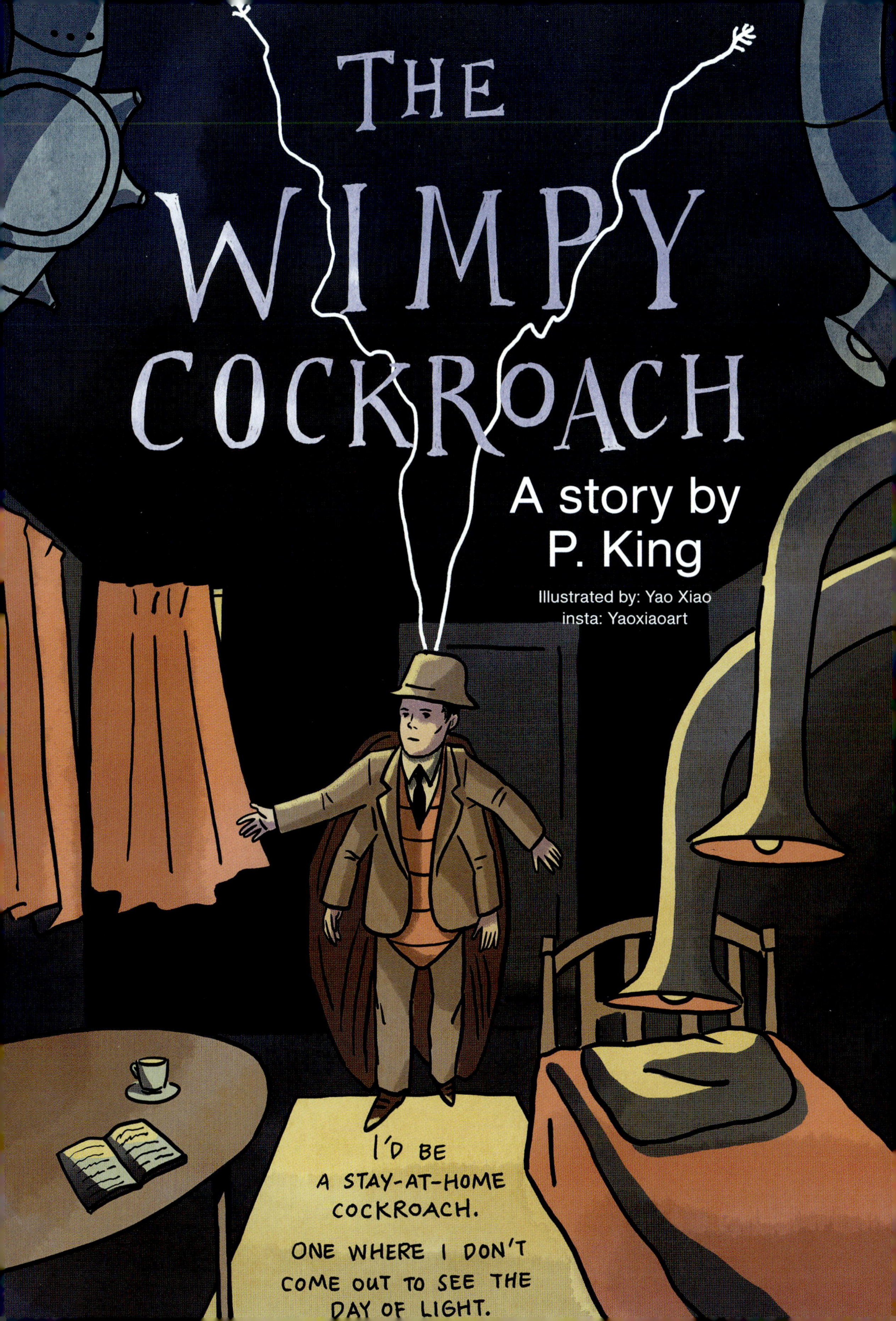
THE WIMPY COCKROACH
A story by
P. King
Illustrated by: Yao Xiao
insta: Yaoxiaoart
I'D BE
A STAY-AT-HOME
COCKROACH.
ONE WHERE I DON'T
COME OUT TO SEE THE
DAY OF LIGHT.

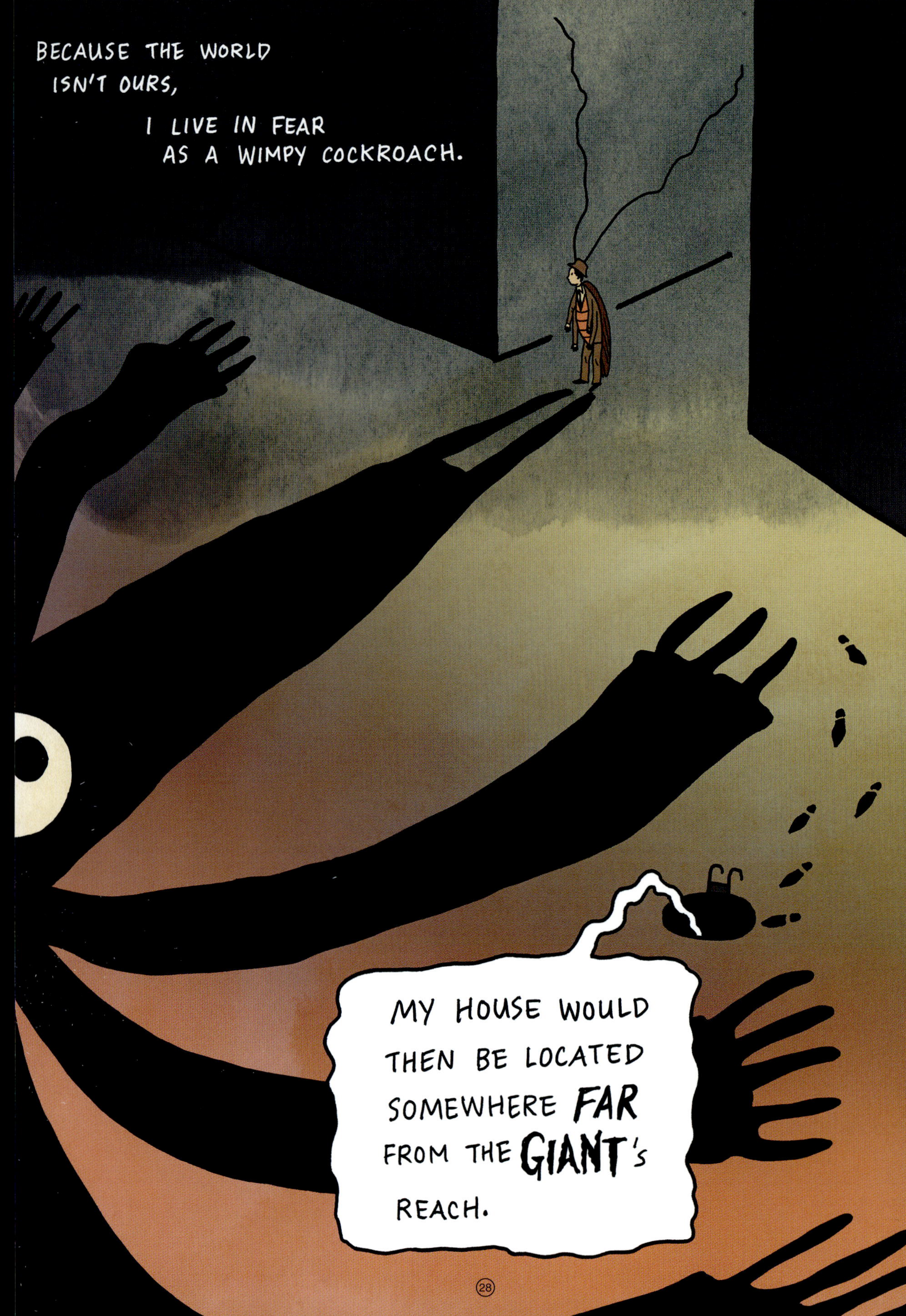
BECAUSE THE WORLD ISN'T OURS,
I LIVE IN FEAR AS A WIMPY COCKROACH.
MY HOUSE WOULD THEN BE LOCATED SOMEWHERE FAR FROM THE GIANT's REACH.

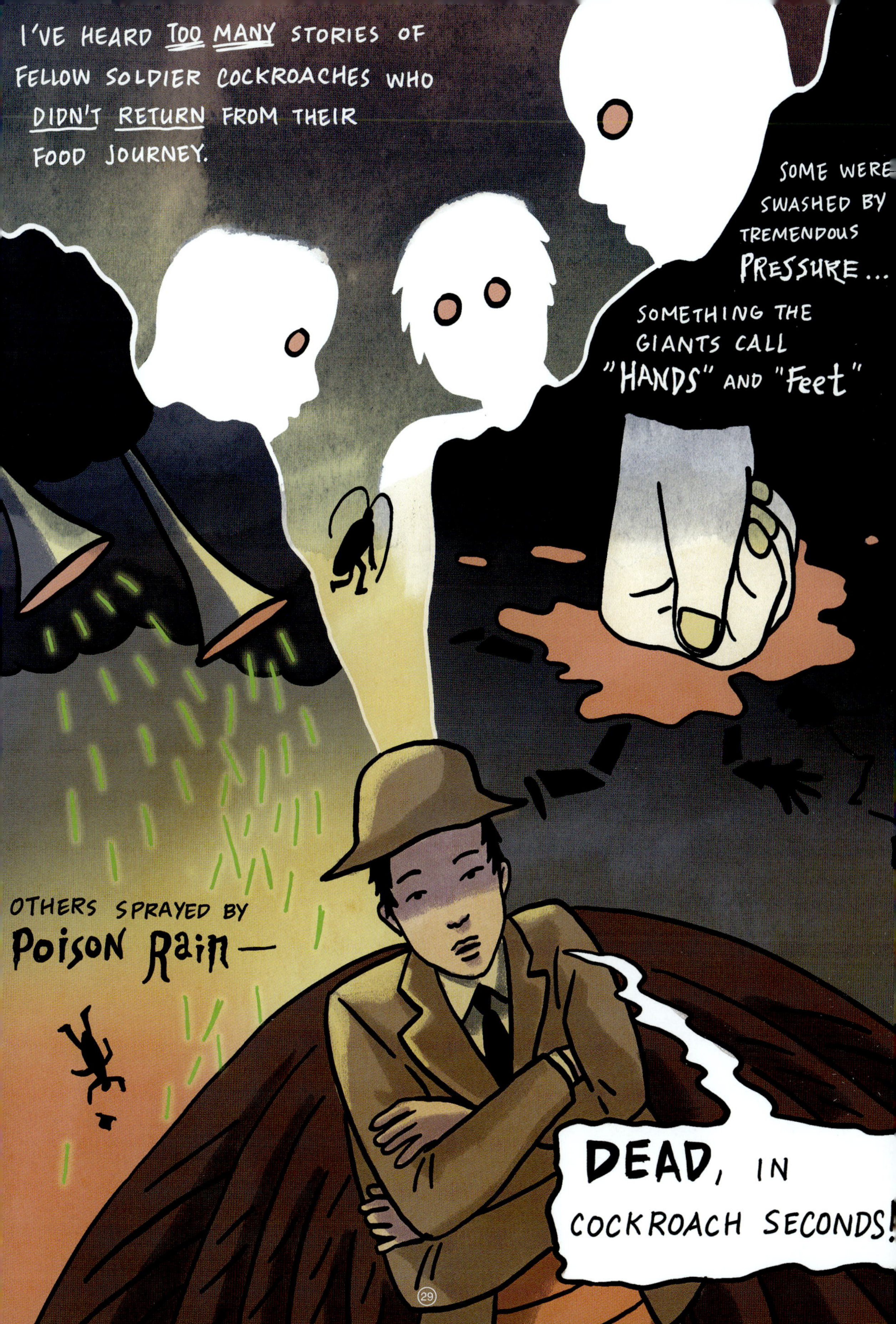
I'VE HEARD TOO MANY STORIES OF FELLOW SOLDIER COCKROACHES WHO DIDN'T RETURN FROM THEIR FOOD JOURNEY.
SOME WERE SWASHED BY TREMENDOUS PRESSURE...
SOMETHING THE GIANTS CALL "HANDS" AND "Feet"
OTHERS SPRAYED BY Poison Rain—
DEAD, IN COCKROACH SECONDS!

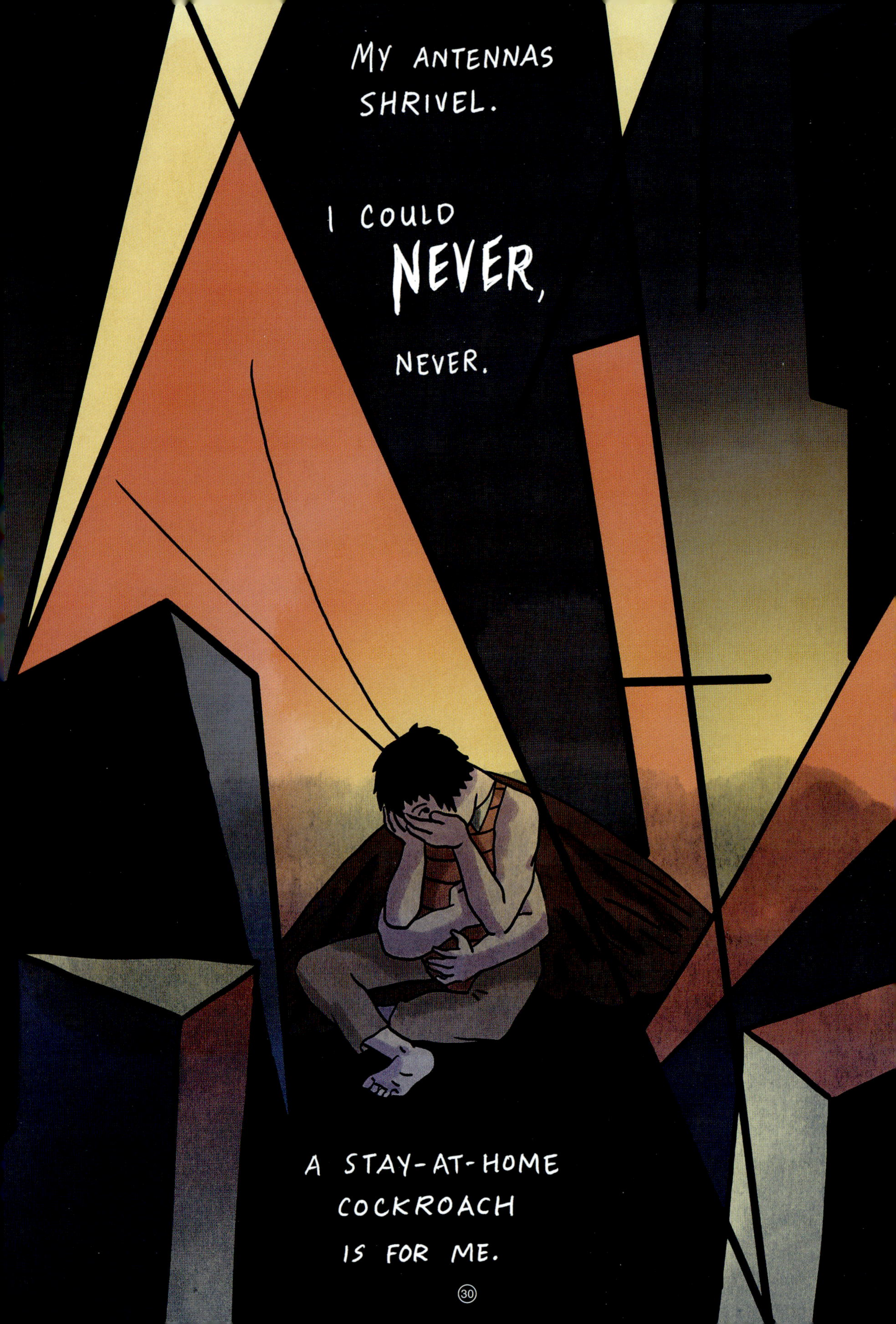
MY ANTENNAS SHRIVEL.
I COULD NEVER,
NEVER.
A STAY-AT-HOME COCKROACH IS FOR ME.

EXOTICA

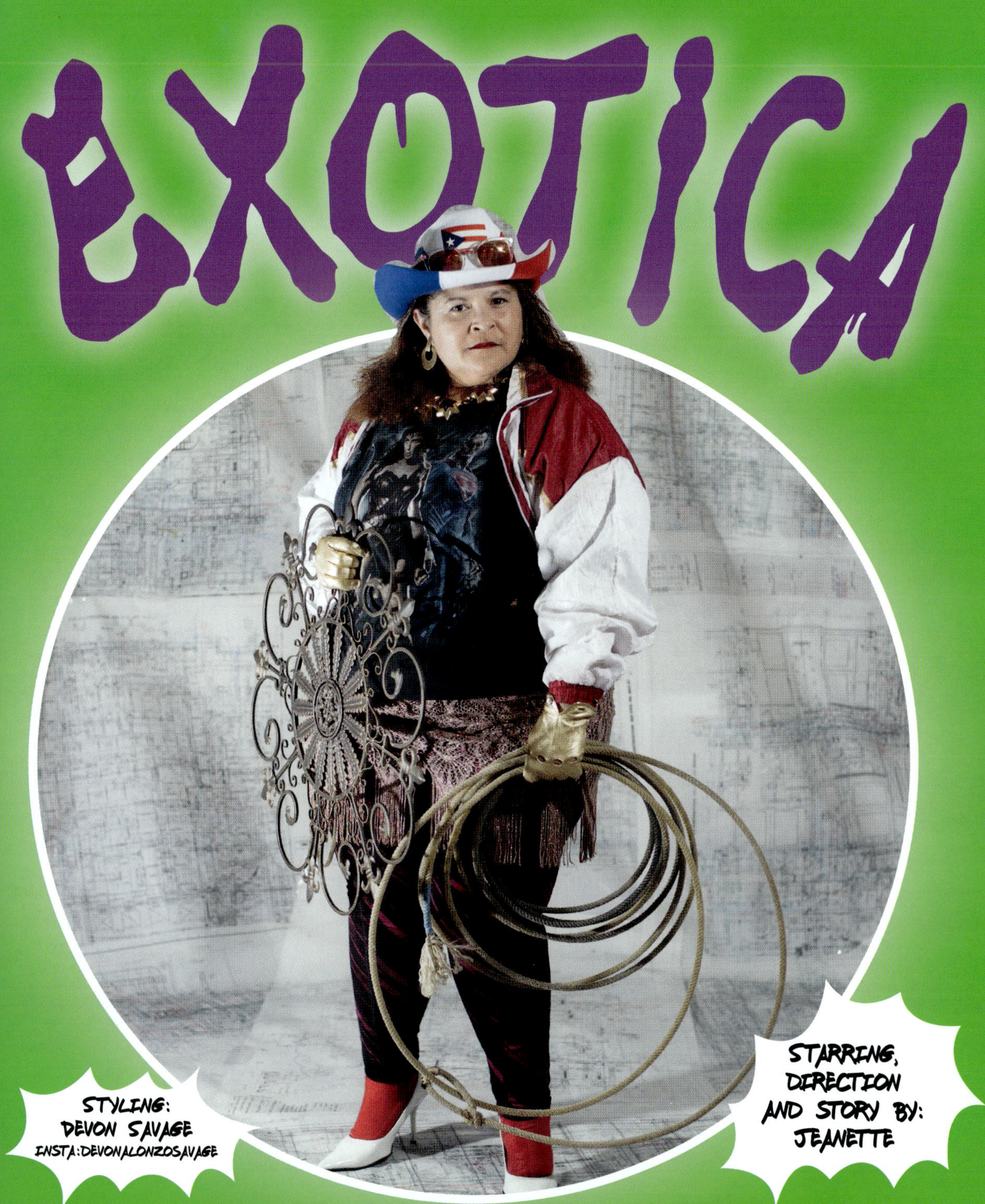

STYLING:
DEVON SAVAGE
INSTA:DEVONALONZOSAVAGE

STARRING,
DIRECTION
AND STORY BY:
JEANETTE

SHOTS:
JAN HOEK

TRANSCRIPTION AND
SET SUPPORT:
WIEGER WINDHORST

PHOTOGRAPHY ASSISTANTS:
JONNA BRUINSMA
SOPHIE SCHWARTS

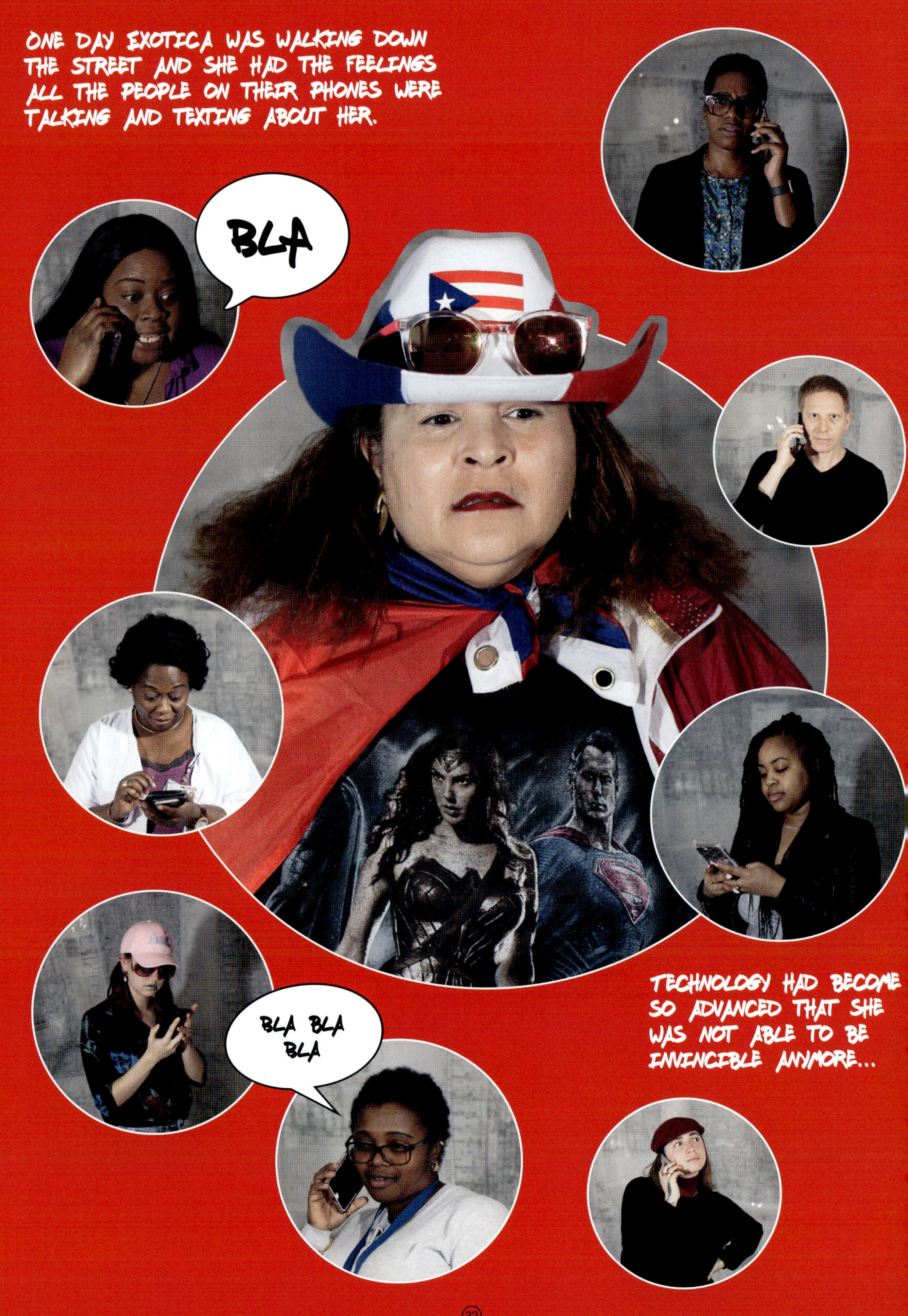
ONE DAY EXOTICA WAS WALKING DOWN THE STREET AND SHE HAD THE FEELINGS ALL THE PEOPLE ON THEIR PHONES WERE TALKING AND TEXTING ABOUT HER.
BLA
BLA BLA BLA
TECHNOLOGY HAD BECOME SO ADVANCED THAT SHE WAS NOT ABLE TO BE INVINCIBLE ANYMORE...

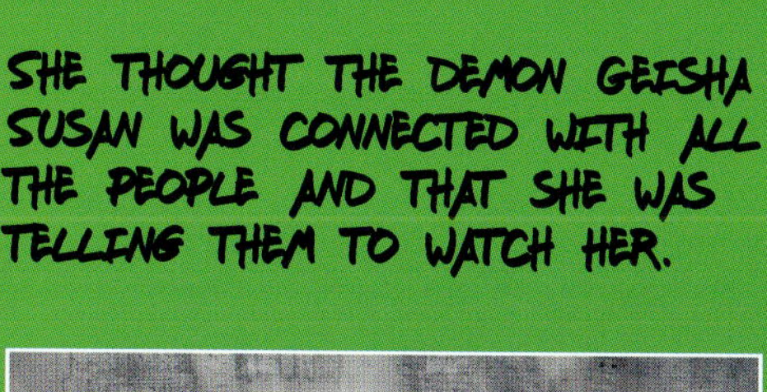

SHE THOUGHT THE DEMON GEISHA SUSAN WAS CONNECTED WITH ALL THE PEOPLE AND THAT SHE WAS TELLING THEM TO WATCH HER.

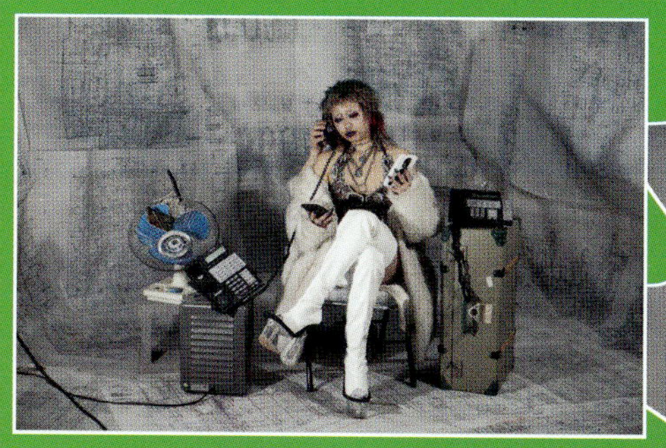

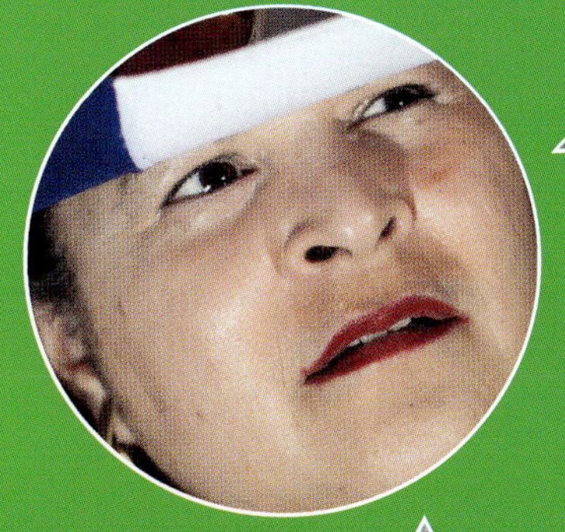

SHE WENT TO CHURCH TO FIND SOME HELP.

YOU ARE POSSESSED BY THE DEVIL!

BUT THE CHURCH WAS CONDEMNING HER. THEY MADE EXOTICA FEEL LIKE SHE WAS POSSESSED. INSTEAD OF HELPING HER, THEY MADE HER FEEL LIKE SHE WAS DOING SOMETHING WRONG. AND THAT'S WHEN THE DEMON STARTED ATTACKING HER.

HELP

SHE WAS TERRIFIED. SHE HAD PANIC ATTACKS. SHE DIDN'T WANT TO FIGHT GEISHA, BECAUSE SHE FEARS HER WICKEDNESS.

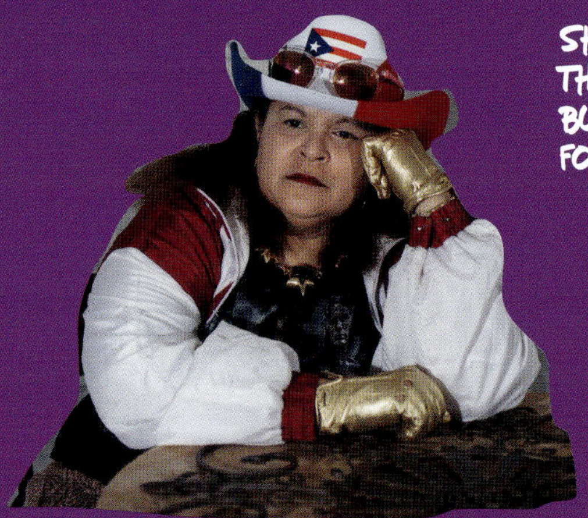

SHE WANTED TO HELP OTHER PEOPLE THAT HAD THE SAME PROBLEMS AS SHE, BUT SHE NEEDED HELP FIRST IN ORDER FOR HER TO HELP OTHERS.

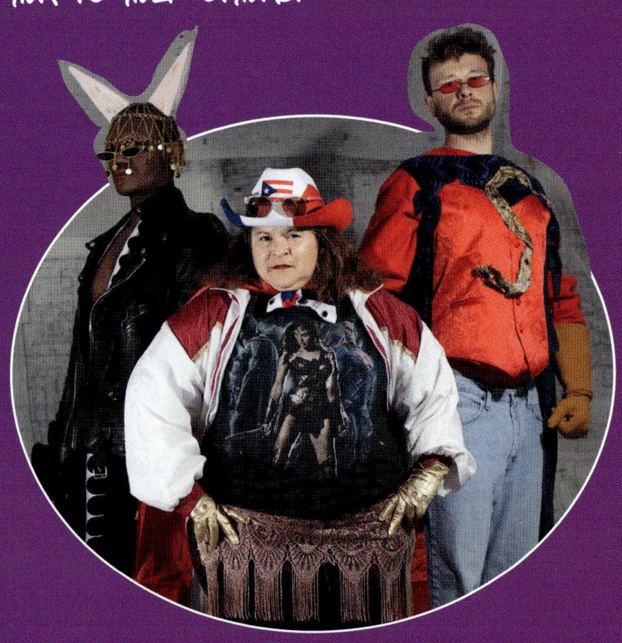

LUCKILY EXOTICA WAS IN THE JUSTICE LEAGUE TOGETHER WITH BATMAN AND SUPERMAN.

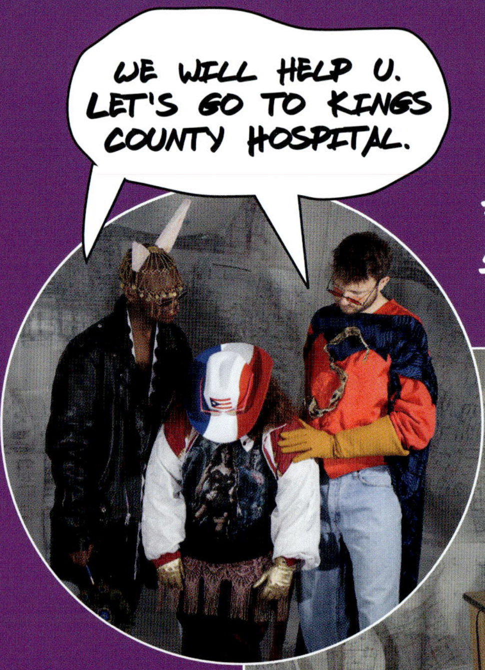

WE WILL HELP U. LET'S GO TO KINGS COUNTY HOSPITAL.

BATMAN AND SUPERMAN WERE WORRIED ABOUT EXOTICA AND ENCOURAGED HER TO DO SOMETHING.

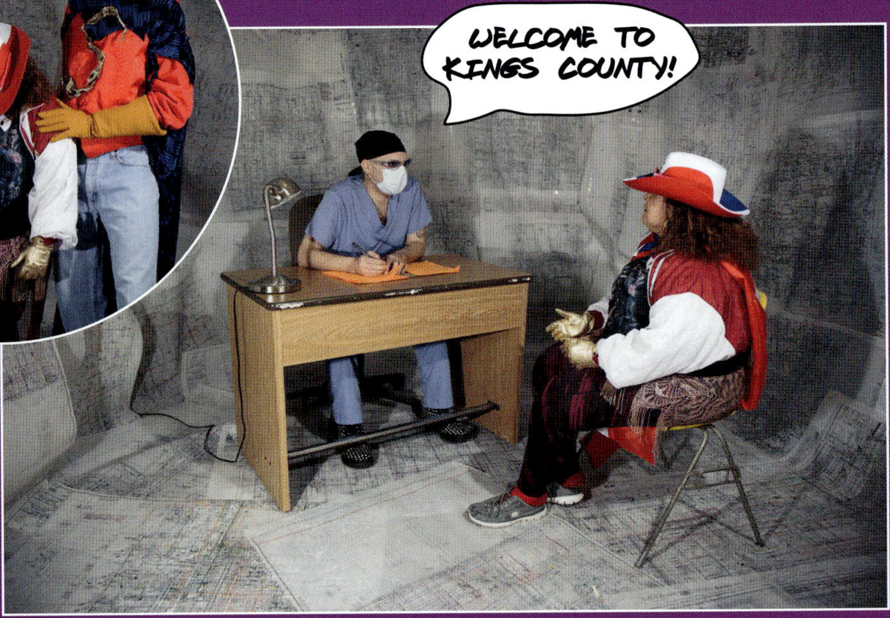

WELCOME TO KINGS COUNTY!

SHE WENT TO A SPECIAL RETREAT. AND THERE SHE GOT DIAGNOSED WITH WHAT SHE HAD. A SEVERE DEPRESSION.

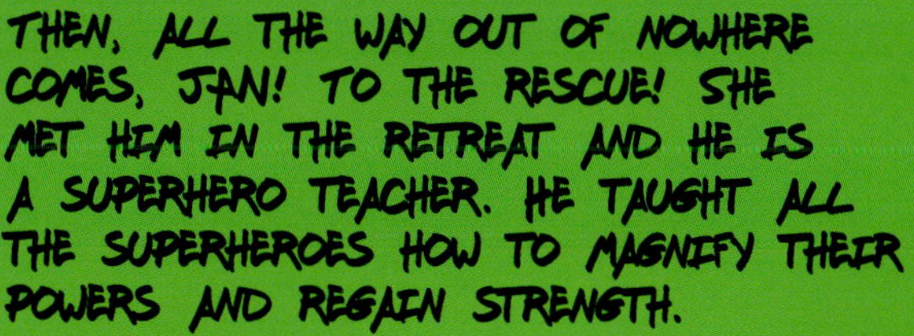

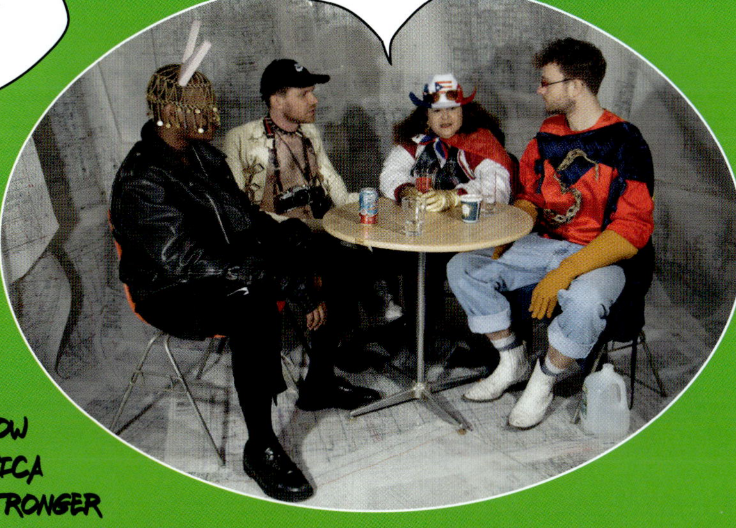

NOW EXOTICA IS STRONGER AGAIN AND SHE CAN EXPLAIN TO SUPERMAN AND BATMAN WHAT SHE HAS GONE THROUGH.

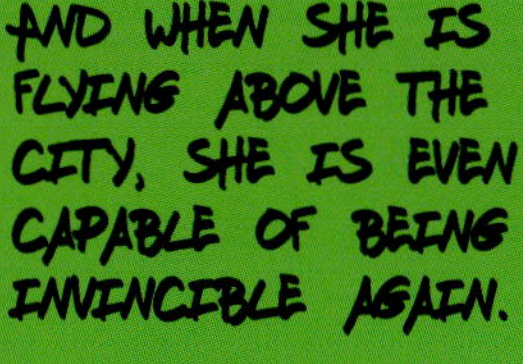

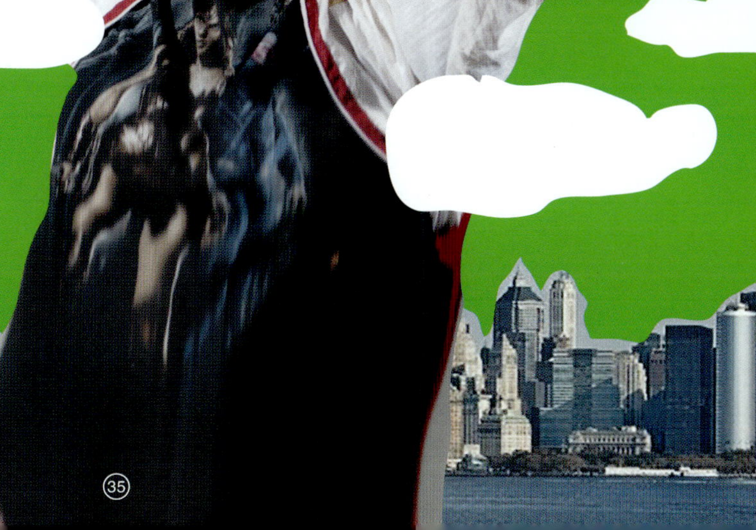

Nick Sethi

I met Nick Sethi, a photographer with Indian roots, in New York. He showed me photographs which he took while travelling through his parent's country of birth.

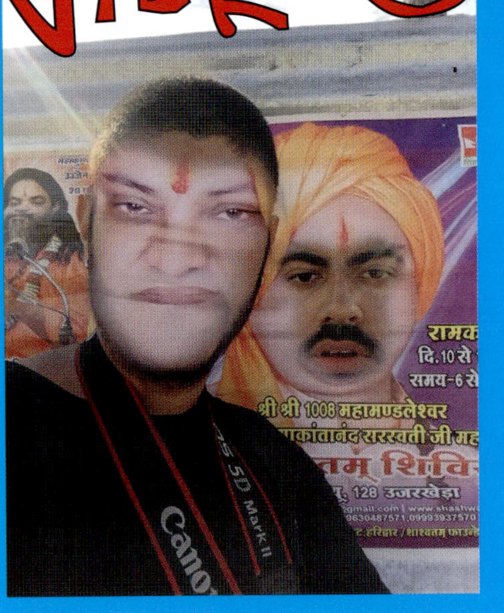

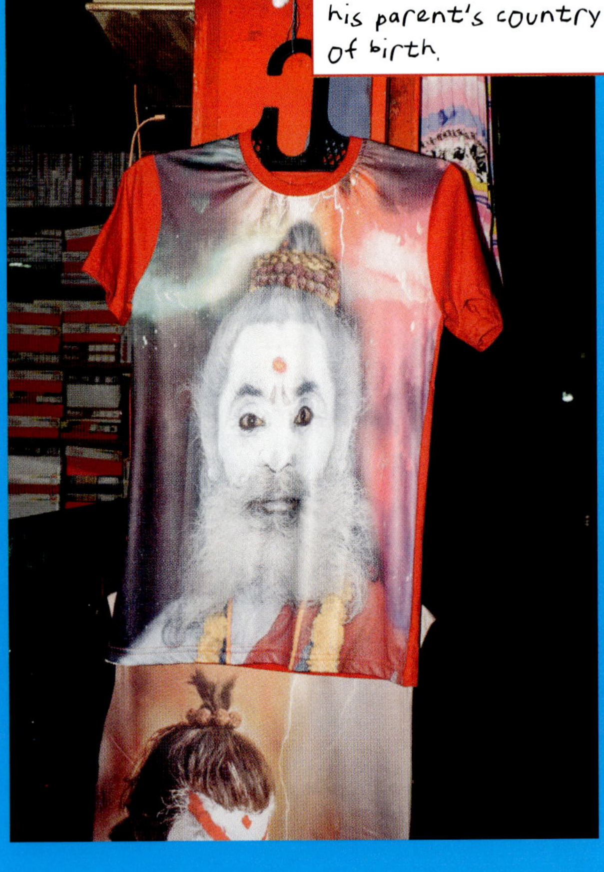

The photographs showed Naga Sadhu's, naked men who would, without a doubt, have ended up in the locked ward of Kings County had they lived in New York. In India though, they're allowed to act crazy, letting it out freely and in public. They're even regarded as holy men by some and live off of donations from people in the street.

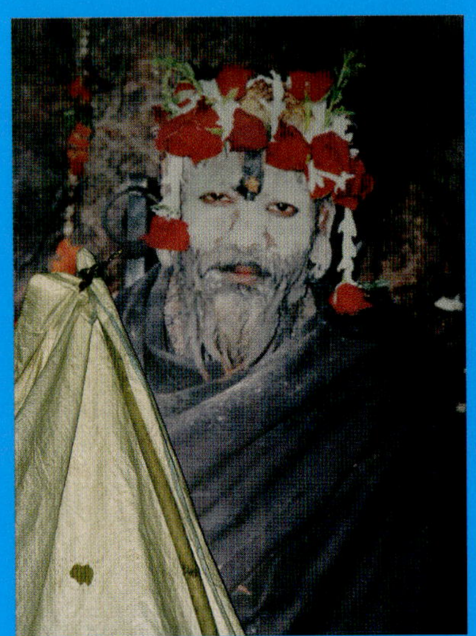

I think of the people around me in Kings County and how they struggle with all the stigmas surrounding their mental constitution. How they're afraid to speak openly about what they suffer from, even in the psychiatric ward; how some were locked up in their houses because they exhibited abnormal behavior; how everyone has lost some friends and/or family and some were ostracized from their church and their work. How much nicer would the world be if all of them would be declared holy too?

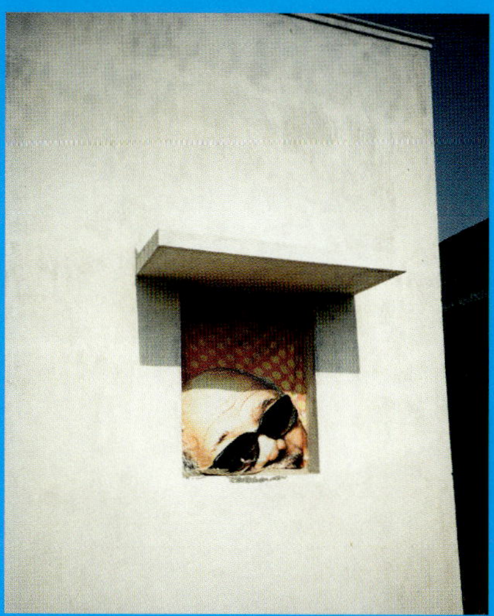

But looking at Nick's photographs, I realize that in America, it wouldn't just be the Sadhus who'd end up in an institution, because, my god, from my Western perspective just about everything in his photographs seems absolutely insane.

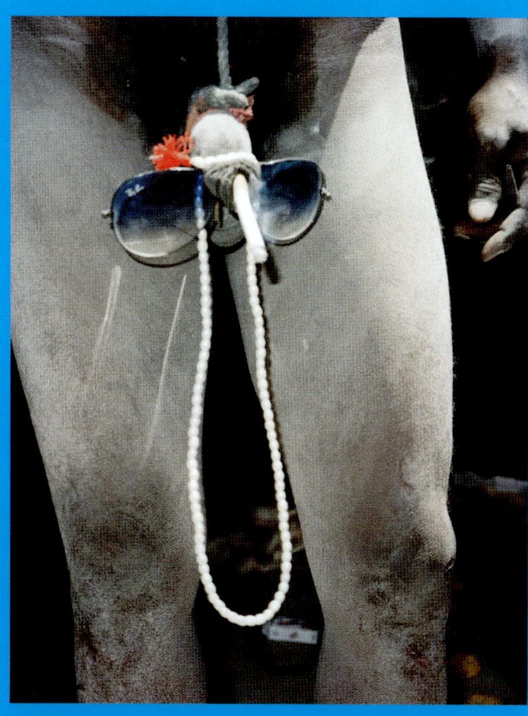

Riding the subway back to the hospital I immediately look up what a ticket to India costs.

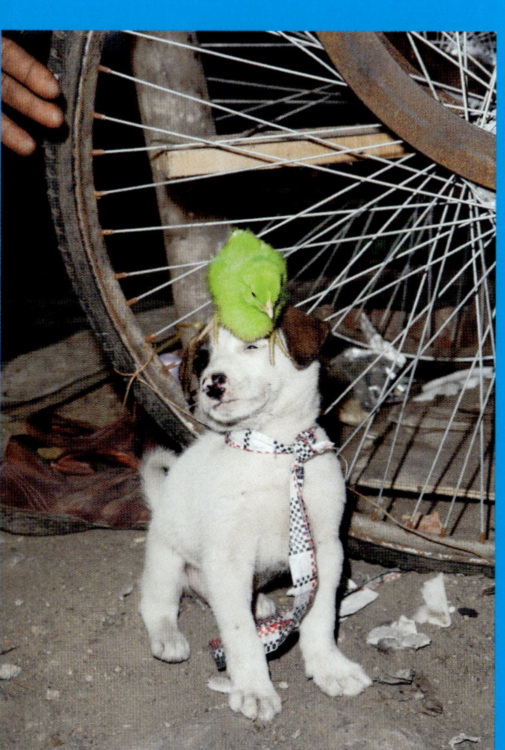

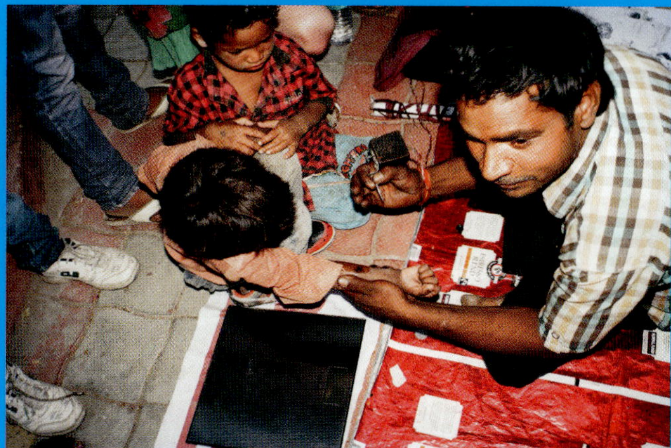

A few days later I'm talking to a gender fluid model from India. "HAHAHAHA, you really think India's that free? Ever heard of the caste system? It's the most judgemental country on earth!"

All pictures by: Nick Sethi Insta: sicknethi

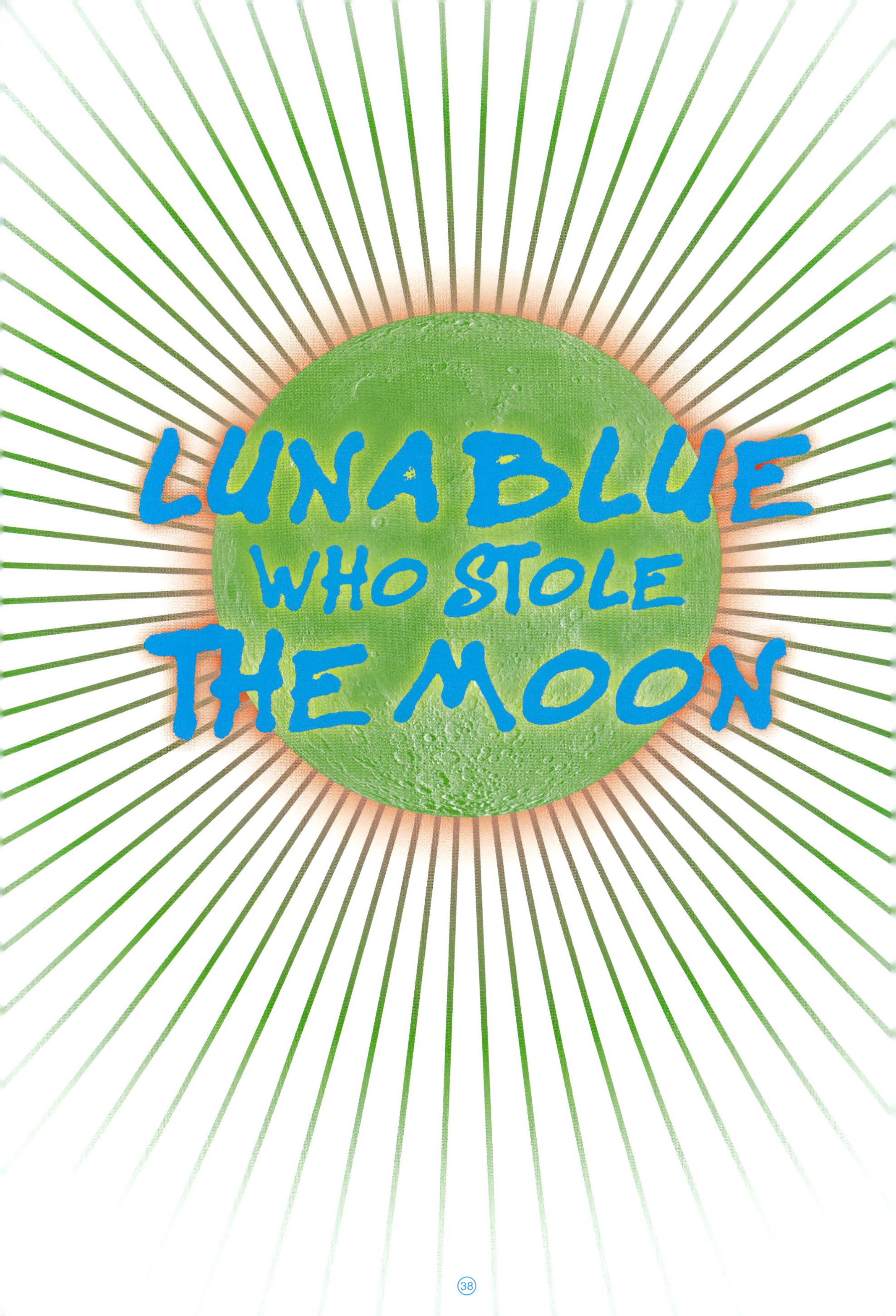
LUNA BLUE
WHO STOLE
THE MOON

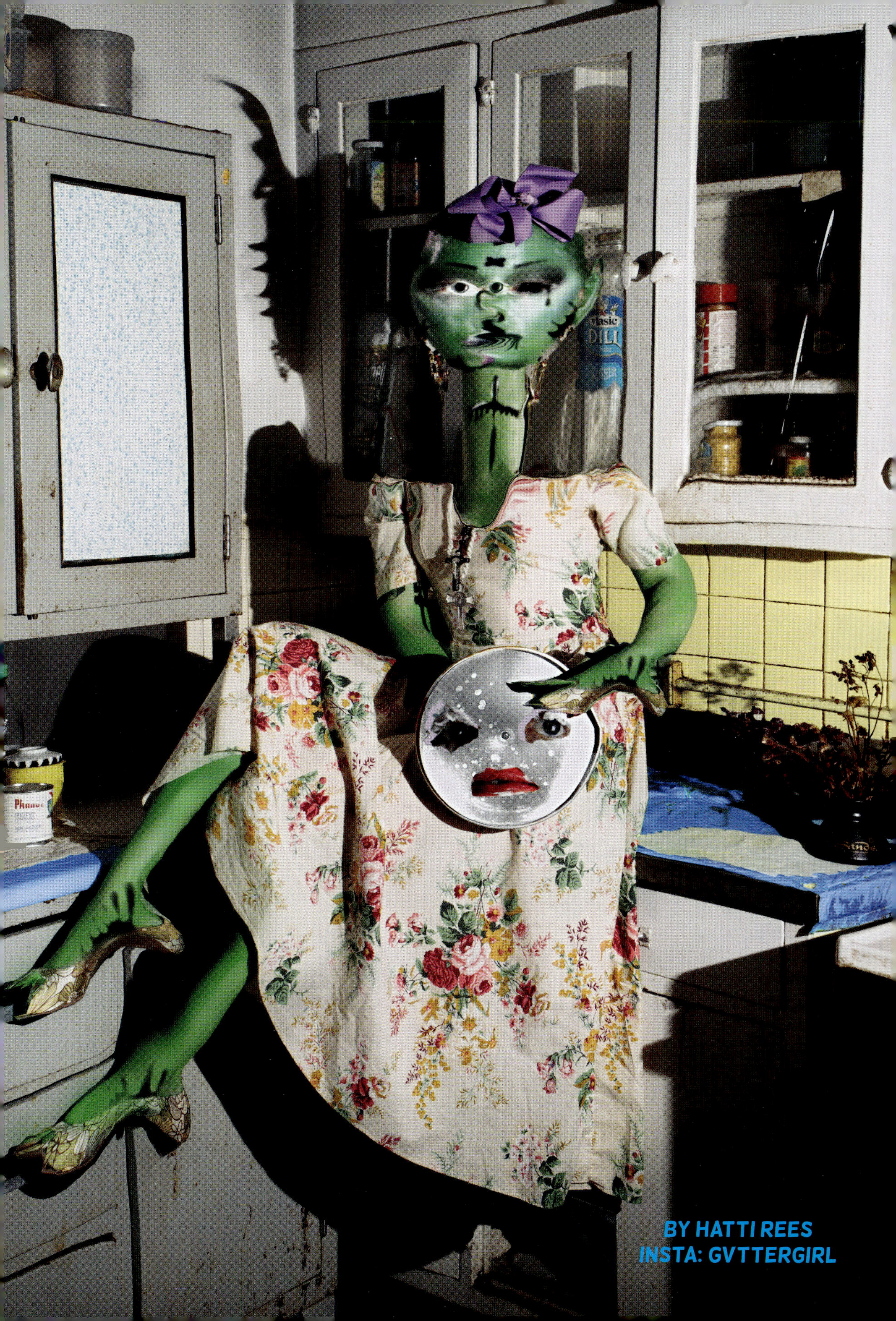

BY HATTI REES
INSTA: GVTTERGIRL

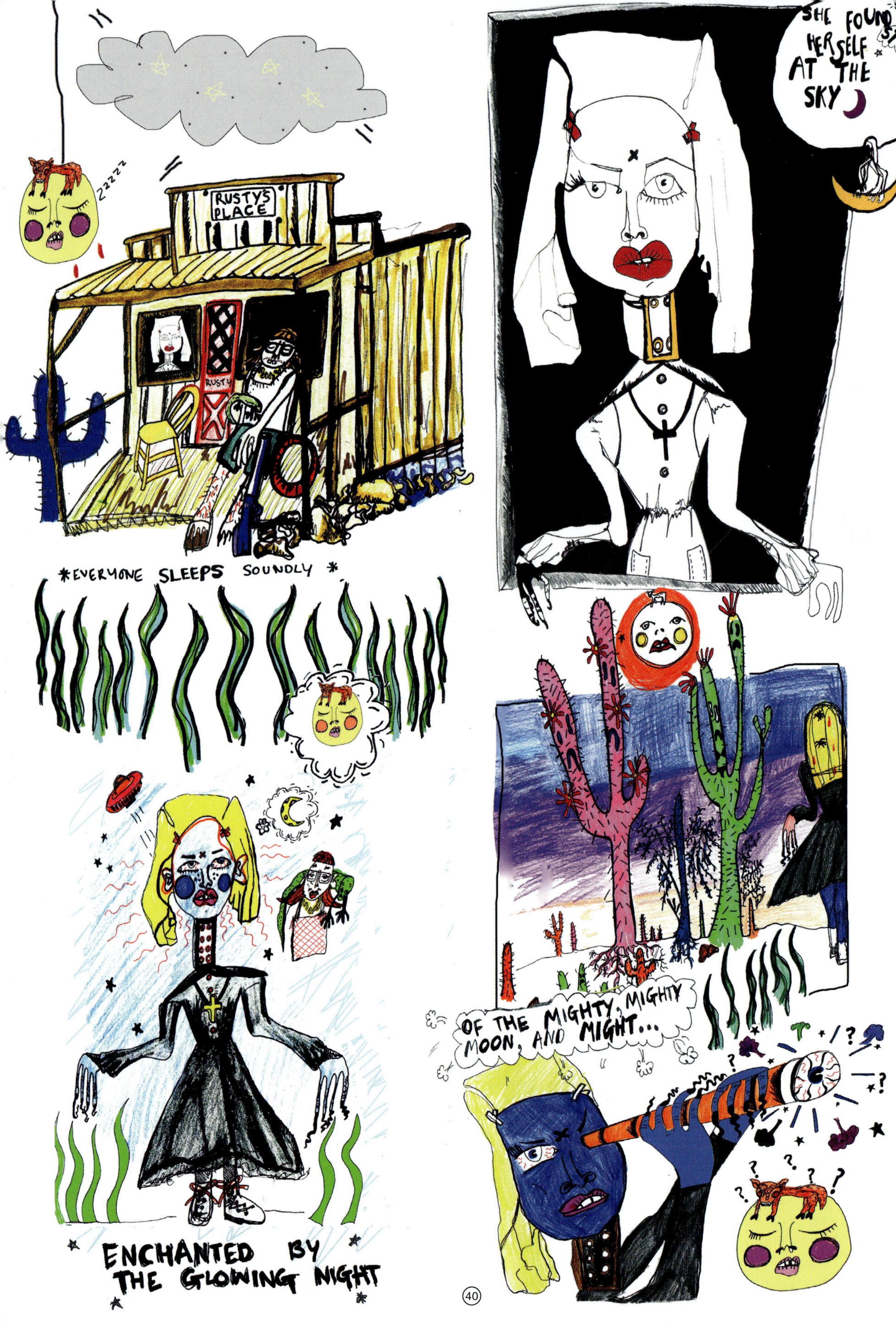
RUSTY'S PLACE
RUSTY
ZZZZZ
SHE FOUND HERSELF STARING AT THE SKY
EVERYONE SLEEPS SOUNDLY
ENCHANTED BY THE GLOWING NIGHT
OF THE MIGHTY, MIGHTY MOON, AND MIGHT...

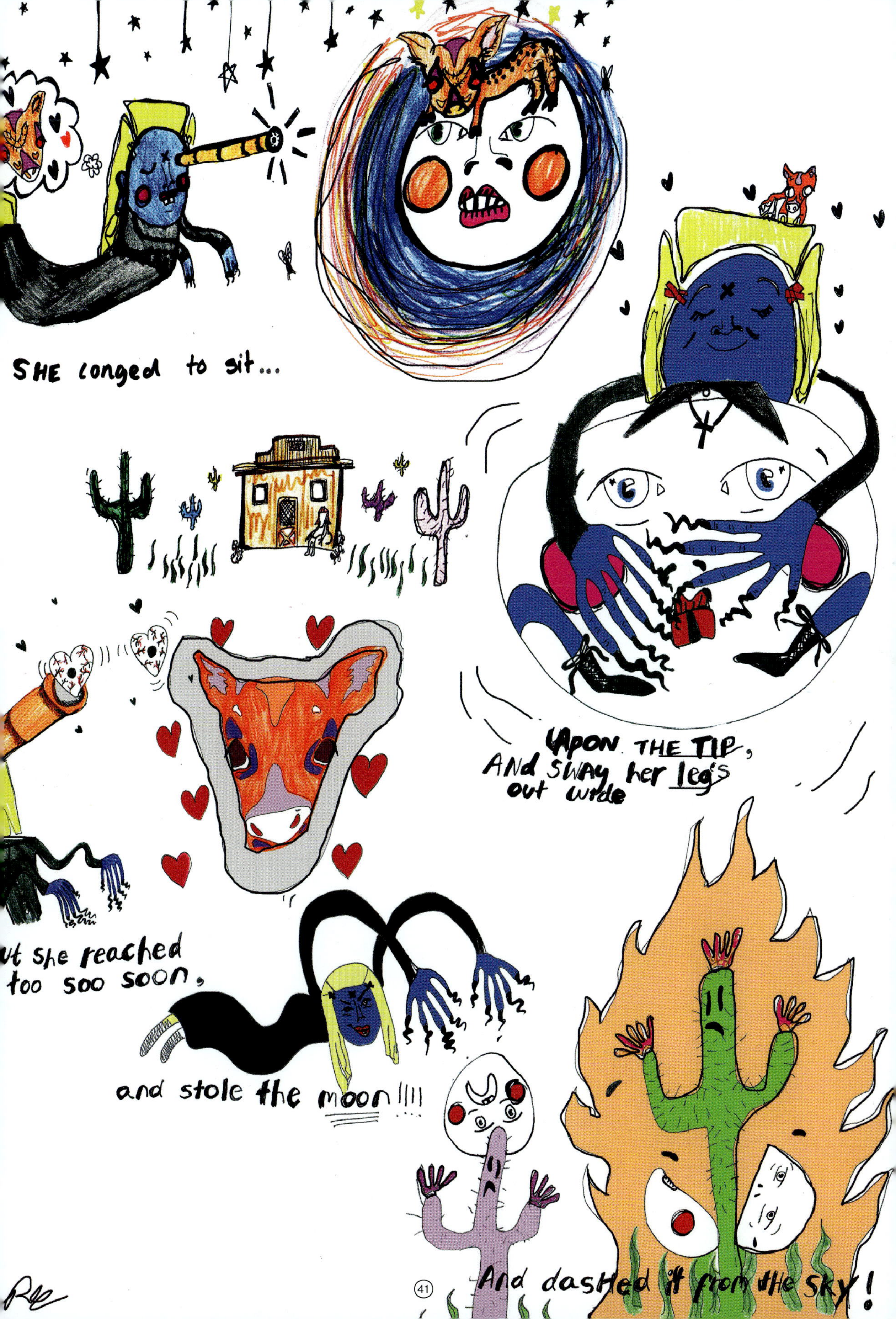
SHE longed to sit...
UPON THE TIP,
And SWAY her leg's
out wide
ut She reached
too soo soon,
and stole the moon!!!!
And dashed it from the SKY!

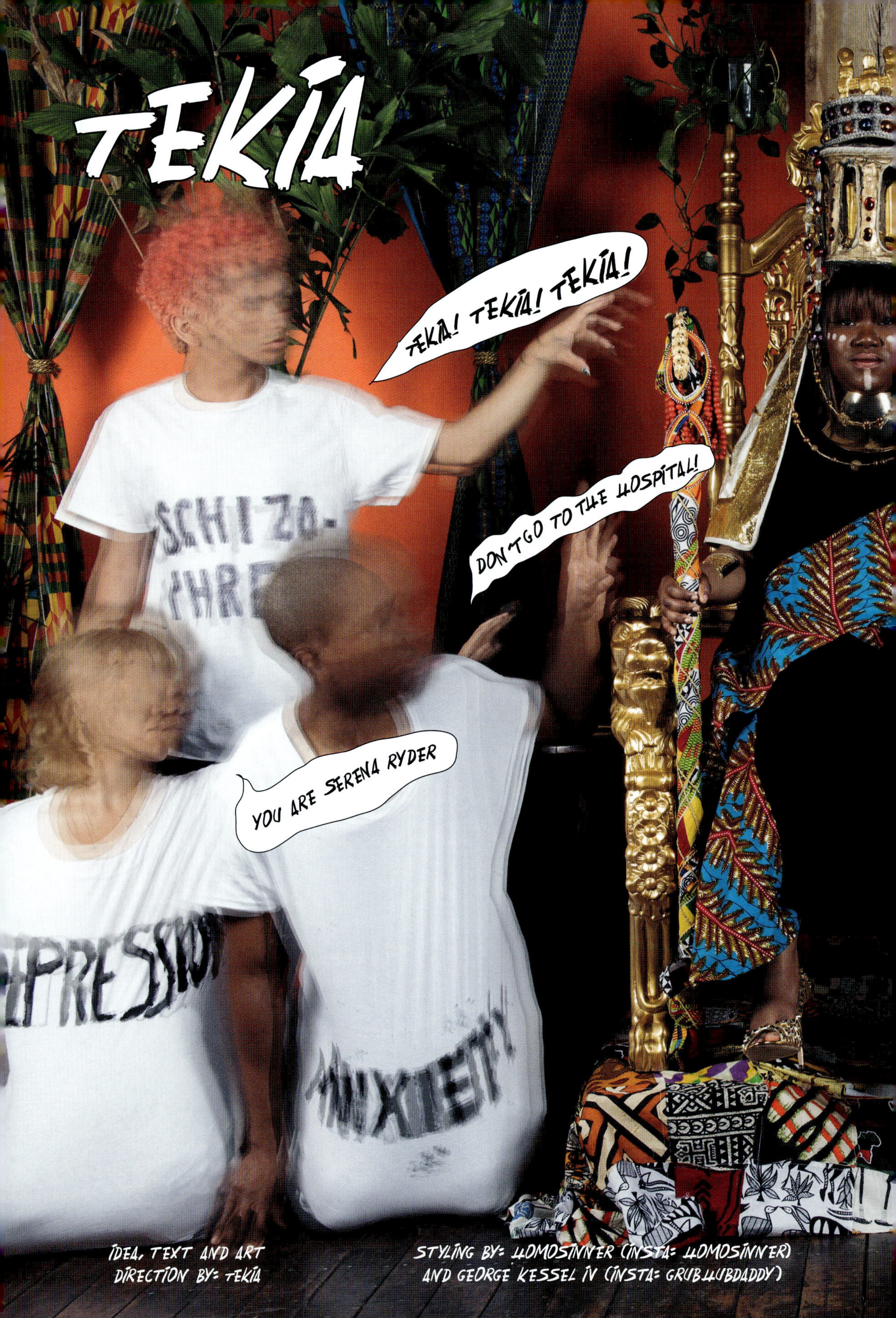
TEKÍA
TEKÍA! TEKÍA! TEKÍA!
DON'T GO TO THE HOSPITAL!
YOU ARE SERENA RYDER
IDEA, TEXT AND ART DIRECTION BY: TEKÍA
STYLING BY: HOMOSINNER (INSTA: HOMOSINNER) AND GEORGE KESSEL IV (INSTA: GRUBHUBDADDY)

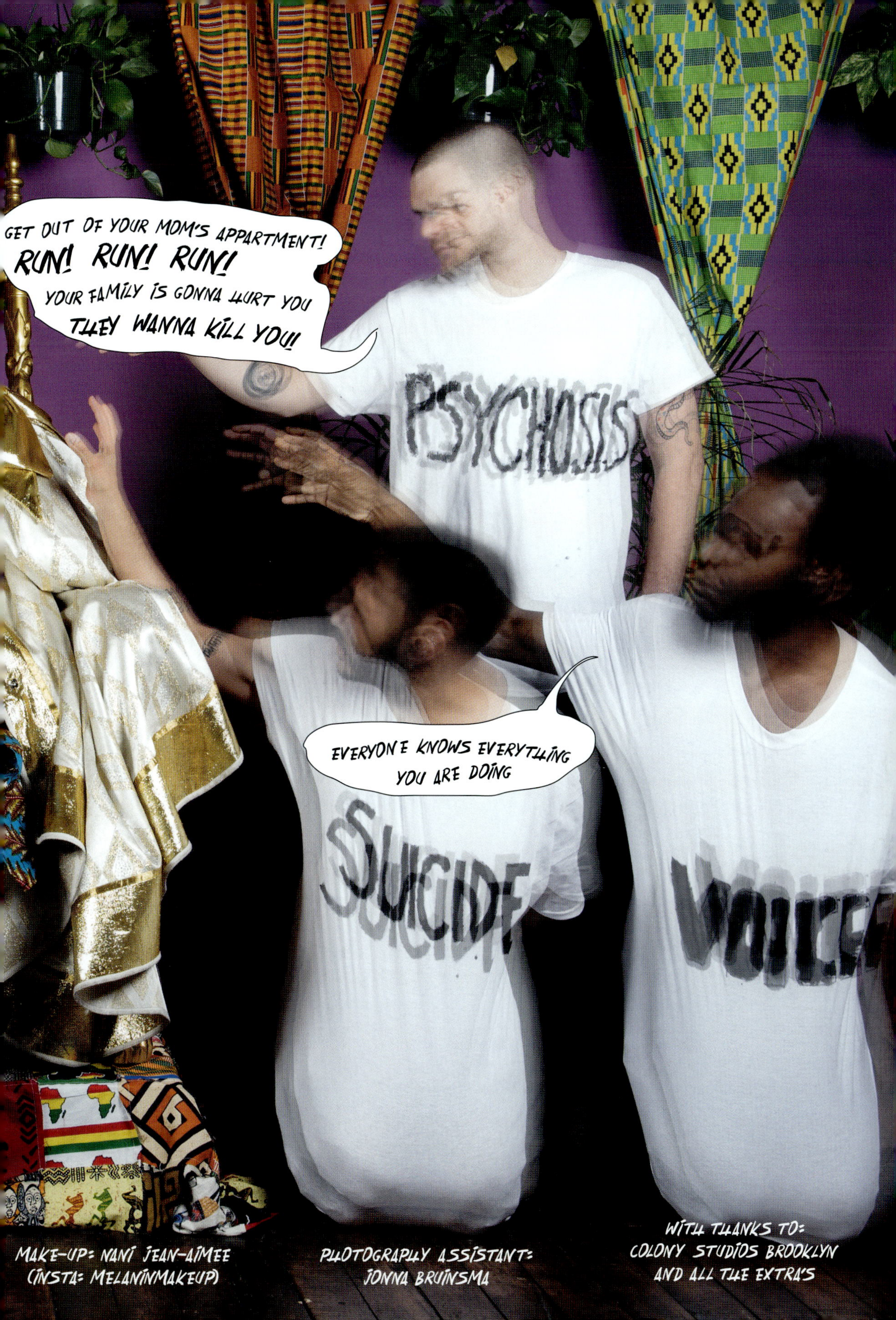

MAKE-UP: NANI JEAN-AIMEE (INSTA: MELANINMAKEUP)

PHOTOGRAPHY ASSISTANT: JONNA BRUINSMA

WITH THANKS TO: COLONY STUDIOS BROOKLYN AND ALL THE EXTRA'S

Why my white skin makes it easier to be mental

For a long time I had doubts about putting something in the comic about skin color and how mental diversity is interpreted. I am white so I don't want to pretend I'm the big racism expert, but at the same time it plays such a huge role at the PHP that I also couldn't leave this issue out. I knew this for sure after riding the elevator with one of the psychiatric hospital's clients.

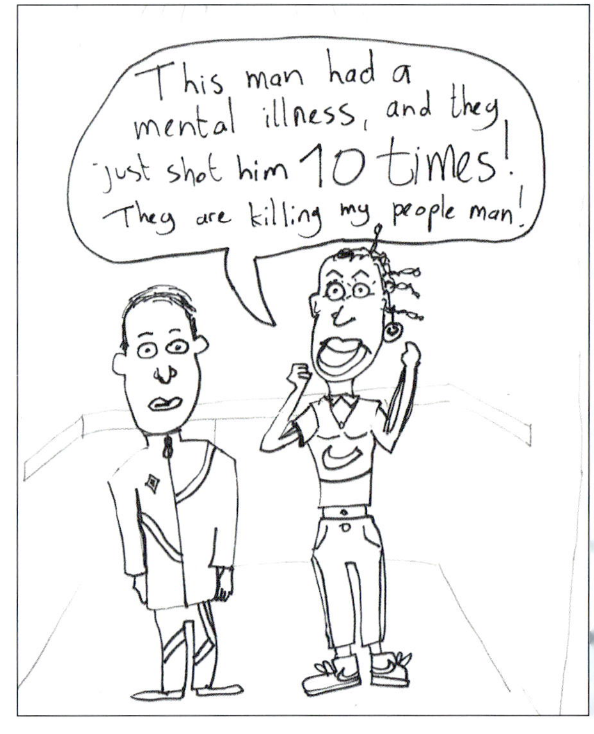

The cops had apparently shot a man to death in Brooklyn the day before. He suffered from bipolar disorder and had threatened multiple passersby with an iron pipe which he held in a way that made it look like a gun.

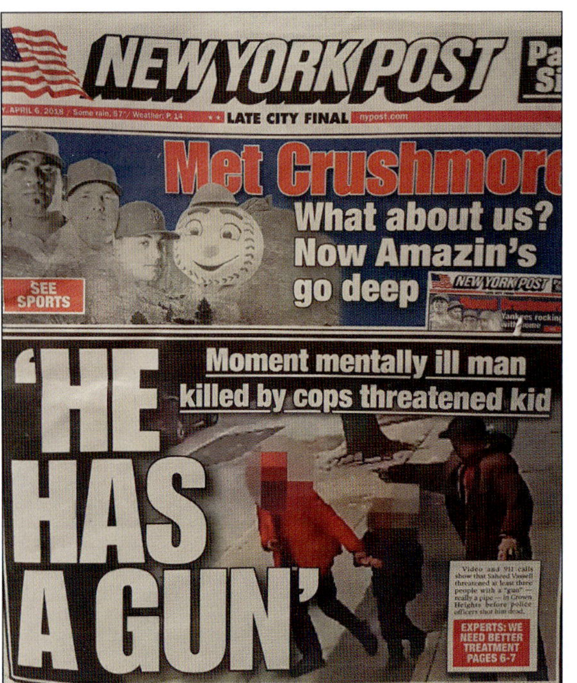

NEW YORK POST

APRIL 6, 2018 / Some rain, 57° / Weather: P. 14 LATE CITY FINAL nypost.com

Met Crushmore

What about us? Now Amazin's go deep

SEE SPORTS

'HE HAS A GUN'

Moment mentally ill man killed by cops threatened kid

Video and 911 calls show that Saheed Vassell threatened at least three people with a "gun" — really a pipe — in Crown Heights before police officers shot him dead.

EXPERTS: WE NEED BETTER TREATMENT PAGES 6-7

Most of the people at the PHP are people of color, coming from all over the world. The whole department felt dejected. Even though they kind of understood the police; the man had a gun in his hand, a gun that did turn out to be a iron pipe but was indistinguishable from a gun in the heat of the moment, and he was threatening random people with it, children too. But at the same time, everybody knew for sure that this man wouldn't have been killed if he had been white. And definitely not with ten bullets.

It became so much more clear to me how much of a difference skin color makes in interpreting divergent behavior. My utopia is a world where everyone can be their most eccentric

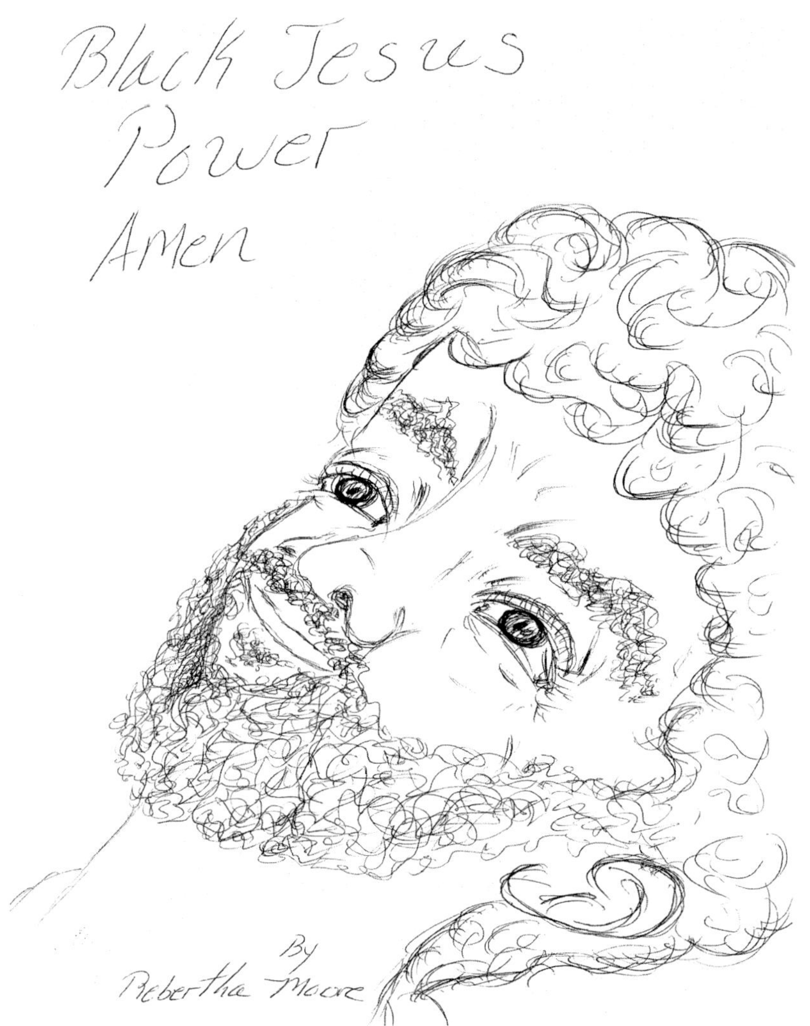

selves, where no one is normal. But the behavior I romanticize has very different consequences for black people than it would have for me, if I'd behave in the exact same way (even though other factors such as class, gender and maybe even physical beauty are a factor as well).
A white man shouting in the street is just drunk, an eccentric or needs help. Someone who's black is easily branded as insane and dangerous.

I met Martina a few days later. She works at the Kingsboro Psychiatric Center which is where psychiatric patients are sent when Kings County can't fix them up and get them back on their feet fast enough. She used to work in prison where she dealt with cases society had even less of a stomach for.
Martina: "Institutionalized racism is rampant in the United States. When walking into prisons, jails and psychiatric hospitals, a sea of black and brown bodies are seen as a product of systematic oppression. State facilities become warehouses for the marginalized. Quality of care, access to care, differs between races, and yet White Americans insist in perpetuating the fallacy of color blindness."

MIRJAM

THE CREATIVE THERAPIST

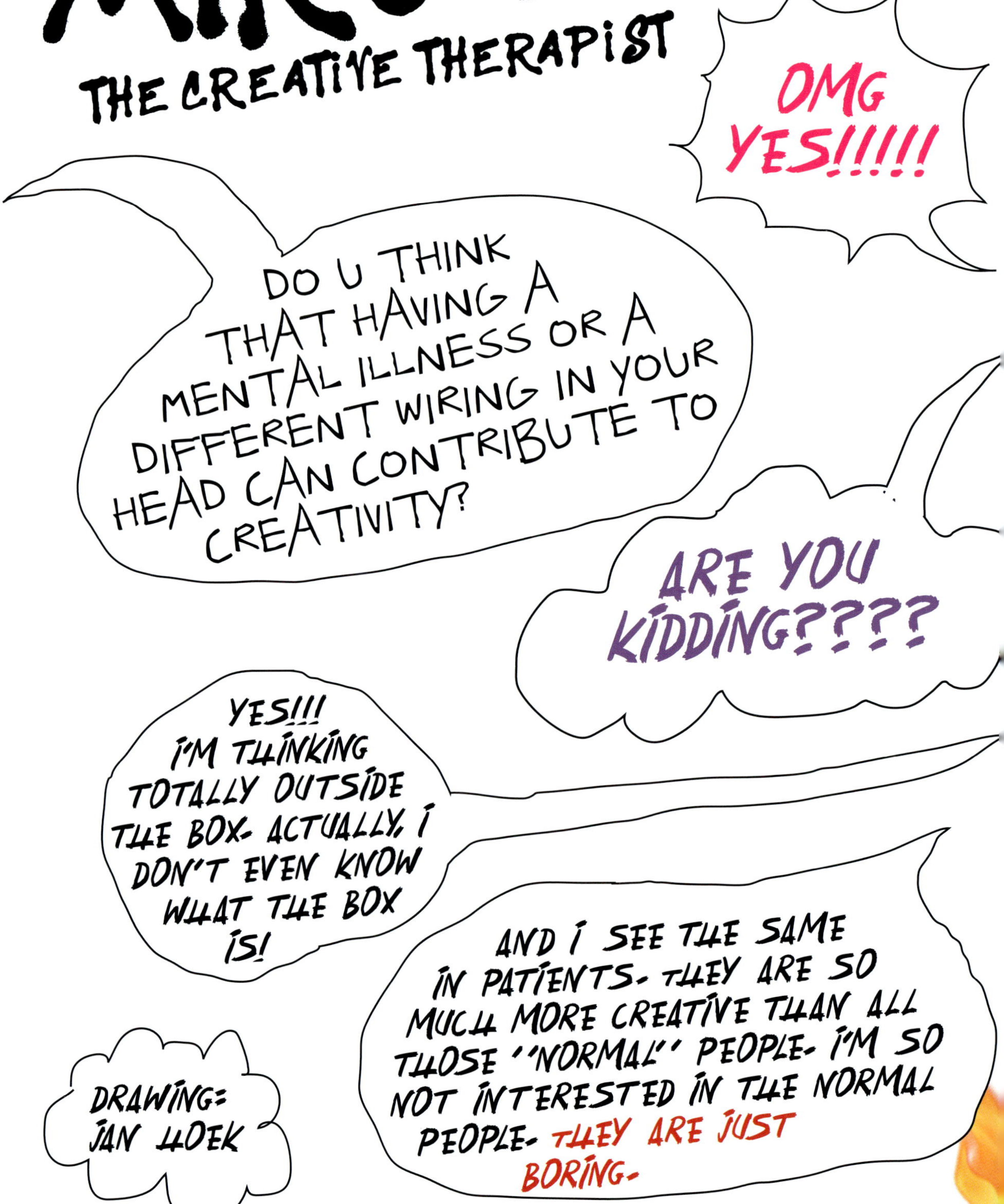

DO U THINK THAT HAVING A MENTAL ILLNESS OR A DIFFERENT WIRING IN YOUR HEAD CAN CONTRIBUTE TO CREATIVITY?

OMG YES!!!!!

ARE YOU KIDDING????

YES!!! I'M THINKING TOTALLY OUTSIDE THE BOX. ACTUALLY, I DON'T EVEN KNOW WHAT THE BOX IS!

AND I SEE THE SAME IN PATIENTS. THEY ARE SO MUCH MORE CREATIVE THAN ALL THOSE ''NORMAL'' PEOPLE. I'M SO NOT INTERESTED IN THE NORMAL PEOPLE. THEY ARE JUST BORING.

DRAWING: JAN HOEK

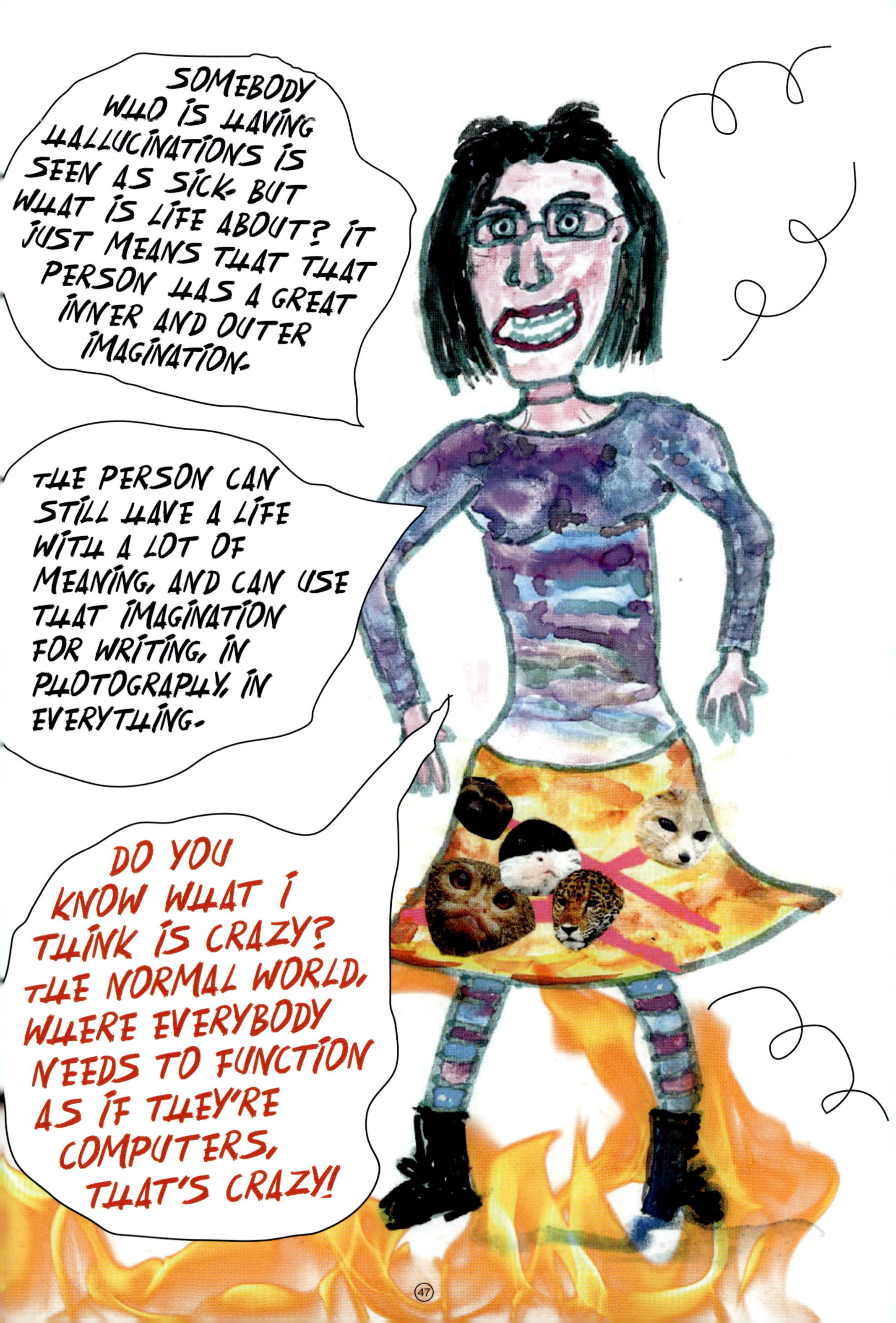

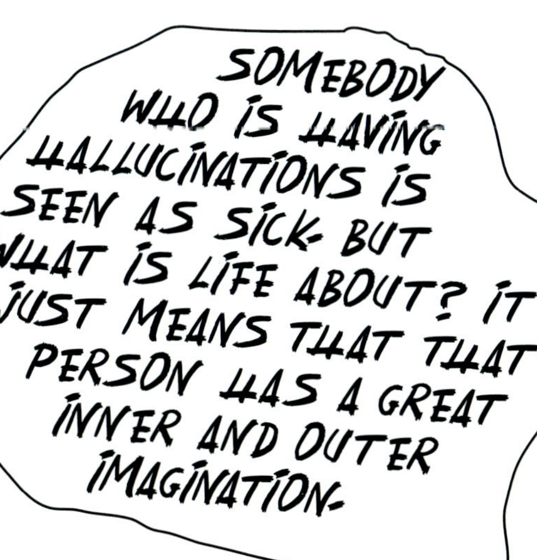

THE PERSON CAN STILL HAVE A LIFE WITH A LOT OF MEANING, AND CAN USE THAT IMAGINATION FOR WRITING, IN PHOTOGRAPHY, IN EVERYTHING.

DO YOU KNOW WHAT I THINK IS CRAZY? THE NORMAL WORLD, WHERE EVERYBODY NEEDS TO FUNCTION AS IF THEY'RE COMPUTERS, THAT'S CRAZY!

Somewhere out at the Sea...

Text by:
Richard Leahy

Illustrated by:
Jan Hoek

A young thrilling black girl, immortal to live infinite lives. With extraordinary abilities of the mind.

Very suddenly she found herself for this journey on a boat sailing the stormy weather... Her mission as unclear as the murky gray waters which she floated on... The cast away ship.

All through this story she was a prisoner to a gang of sailors on a ship which she later believed (although never explicitly admitted) to be of pirates. It was a massive ship of oak and birch. Big enough to take on an entire city block.

Her superpowers were her ability to synchronize minds and assume the correct outcomes of any given task. But due to the unfamiliar environment her powers were weakened.

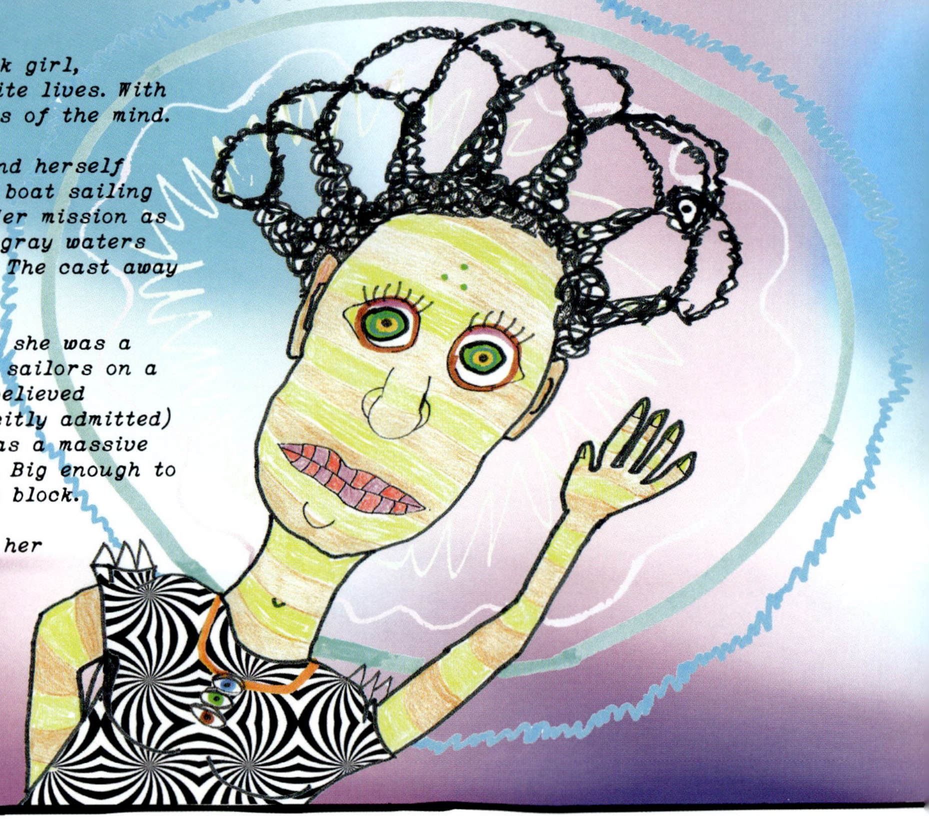

And her only joys in life were to give and share her feelings with others. It strengthened her superpowers of synchronicity.

The ship harbored a small gang of shape shifting sailors. Each time they shape shifted it impeded her abilities to meld with the minds of the sailors.

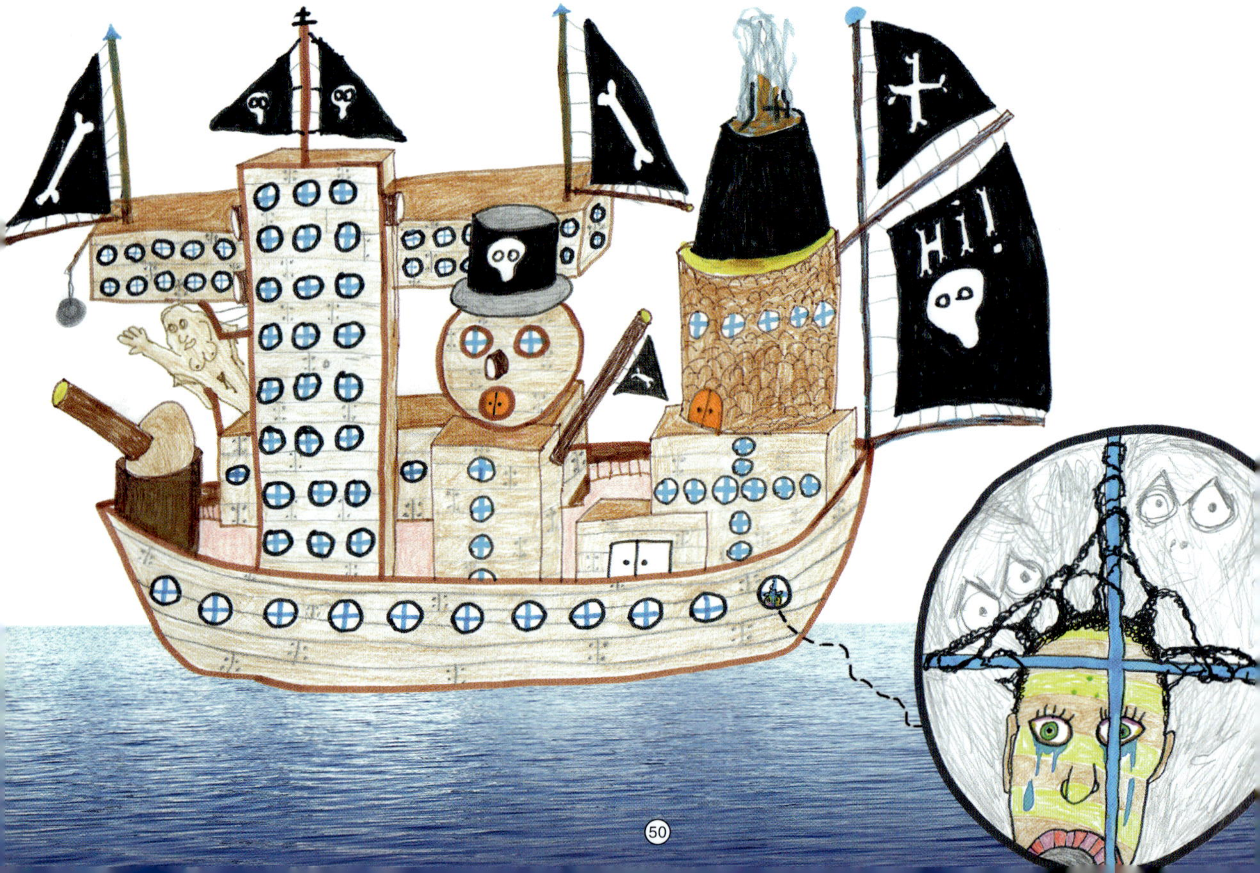

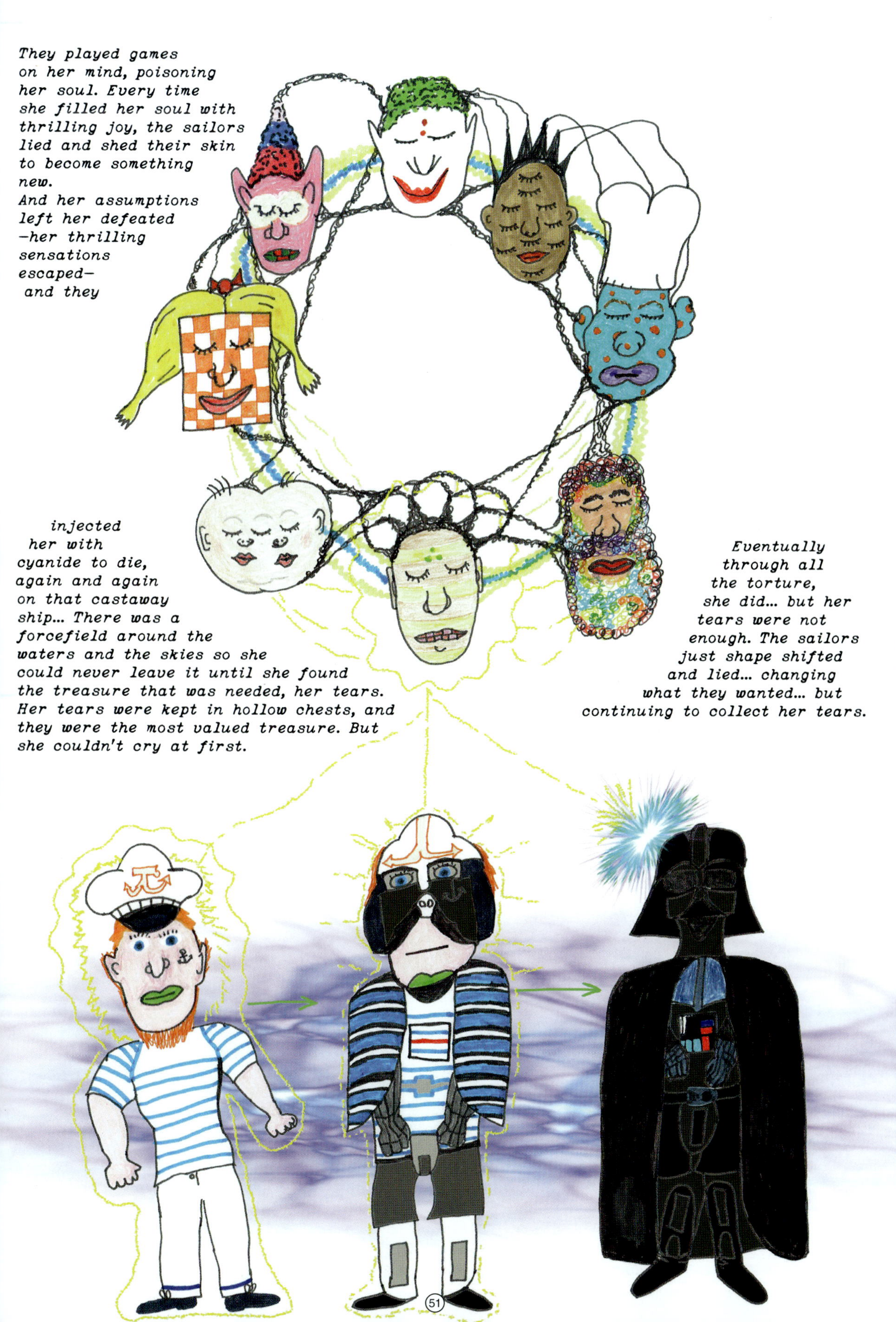

They played games on her mind, poisoning her soul. Every time she filled her soul with thrilling joy, the sailors lied and shed their skin to become something new.
And her assumptions left her defeated —her thrilling sensations escaped— and they

injected her with cyanide to die, again and again on that castaway ship... There was a forcefield around the waters and the skies so she could never leave it until she found the treasure that was needed, her tears. Her tears were kept in hollow chests, and they were the most valued treasure. But she couldn't cry at first.

Eventually through all the torture, she did... but her tears were not enough. The sailors just shape shifted and lied... changing what they wanted... but continuing to collect her tears.

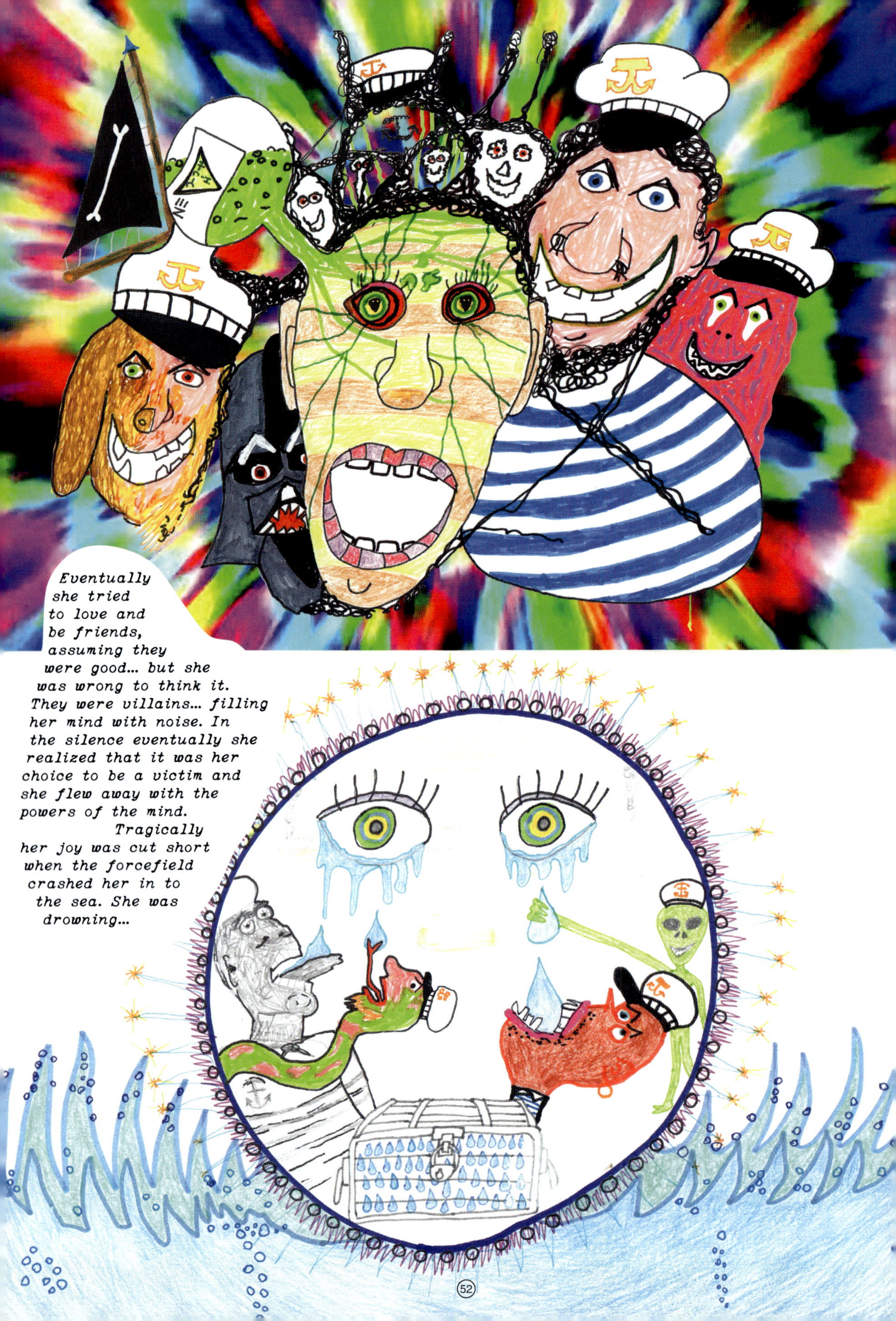
Eventually she tried to love and be friends, assuming they were good... but she was wrong to think it. They were villains... filling her mind with noise. In the silence eventually she realized that it was her choice to be a victim and she flew away with the powers of the mind.
Tragically her joy was cut short when the forcefield crashed her in to the sea. She was drowning...

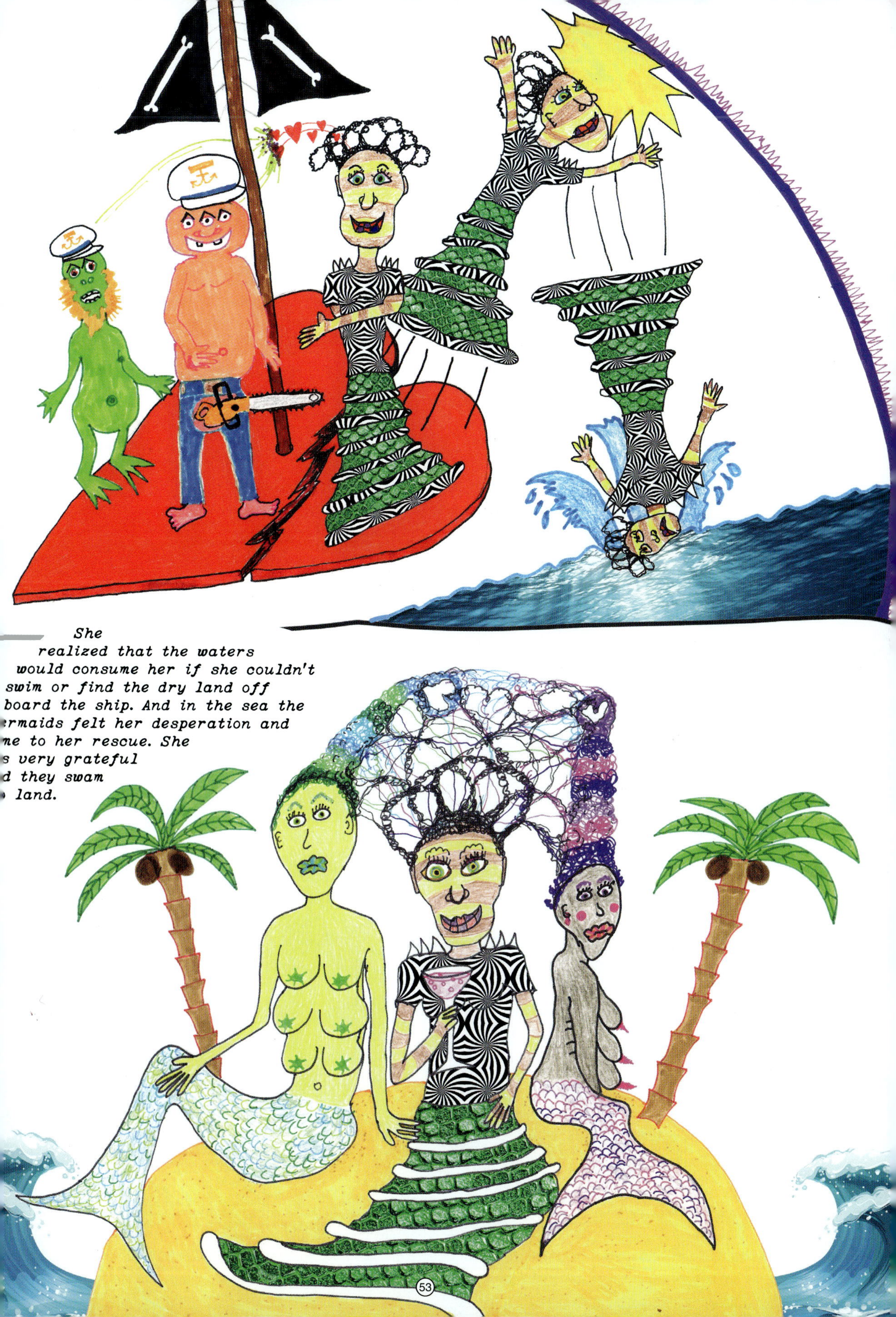

She realized that the waters would consume her if she couldn't swim or find the dry land off board the ship. And in the sea the ermaids felt her desperation and me to her rescue. She s very grateful d they swam land.

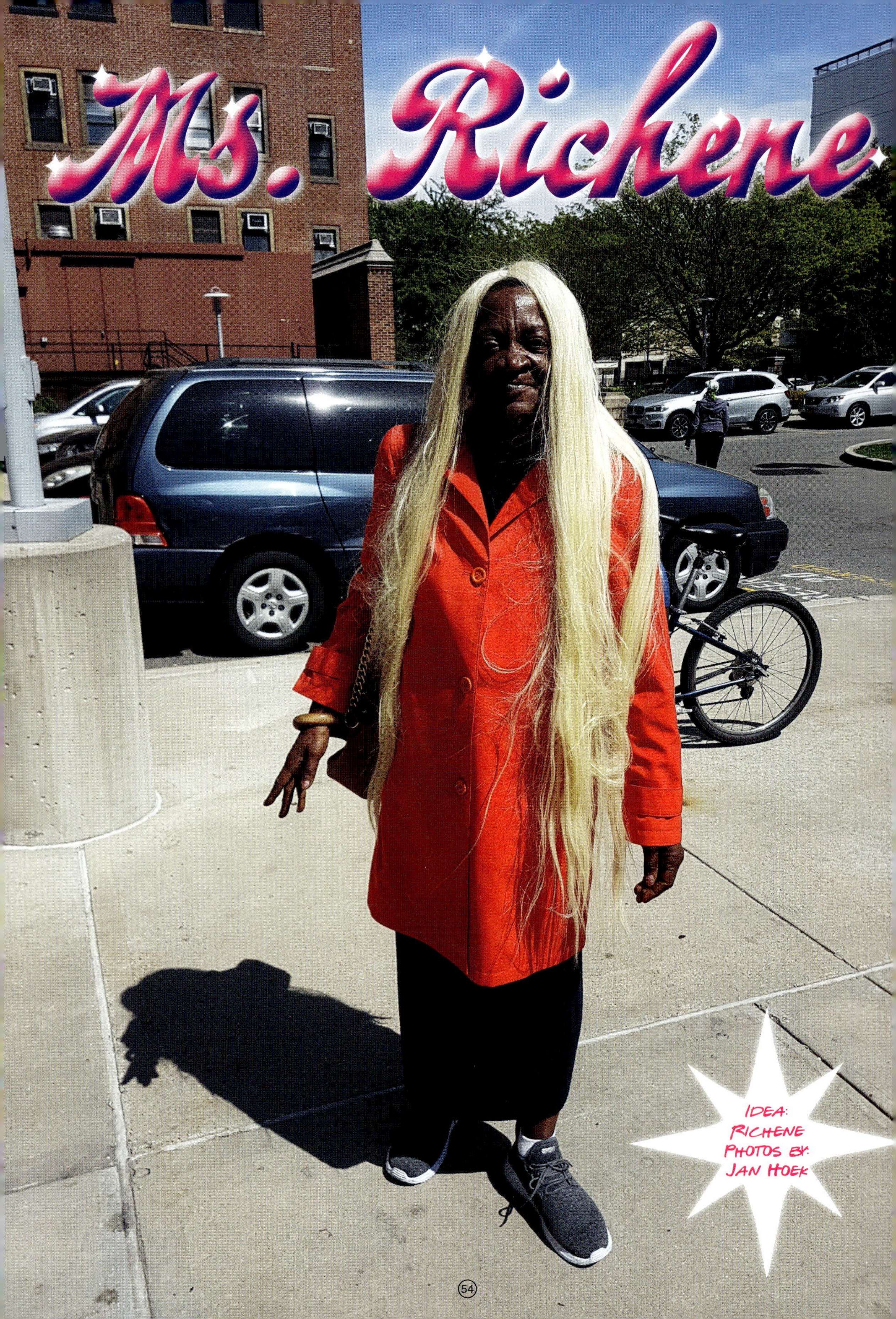
Ms. Richene
IDEA:
RICHENE
PHOTOS BY:
JAN HOEK

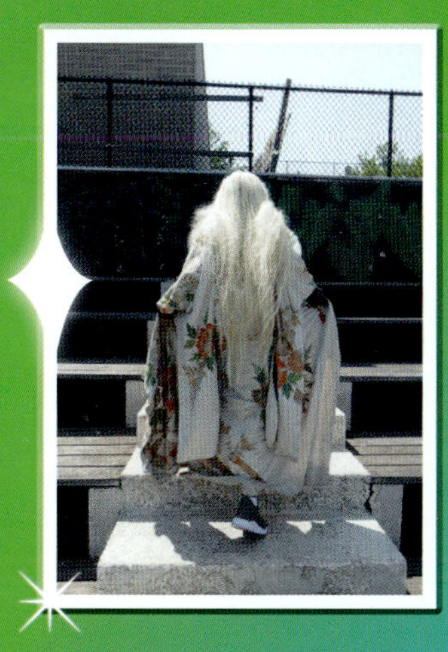
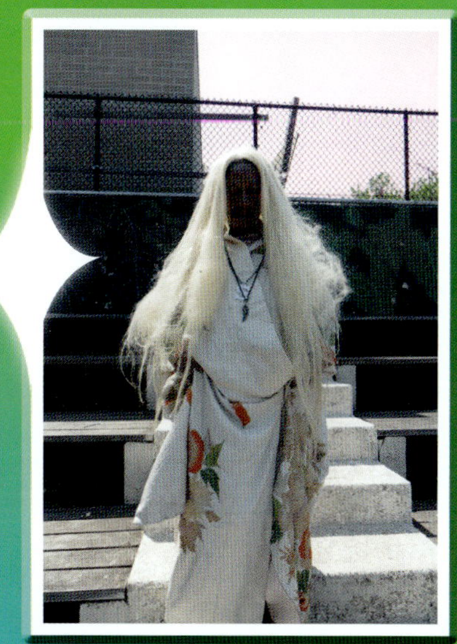
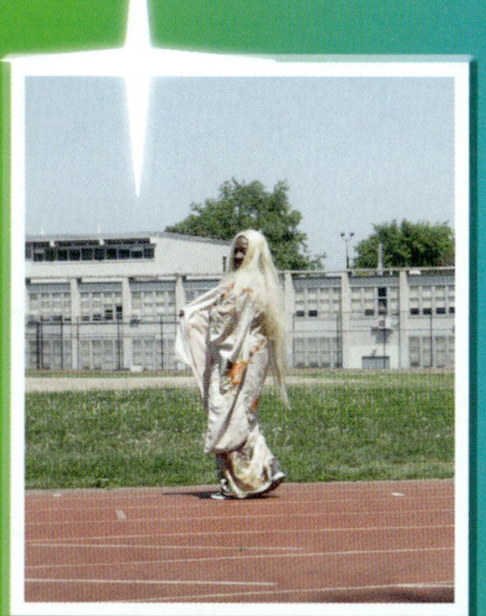
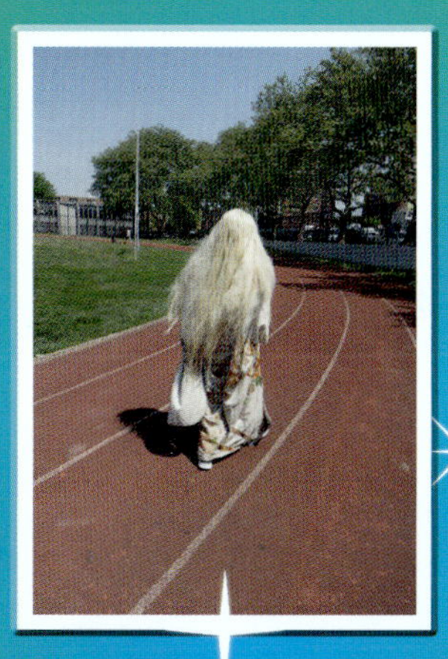
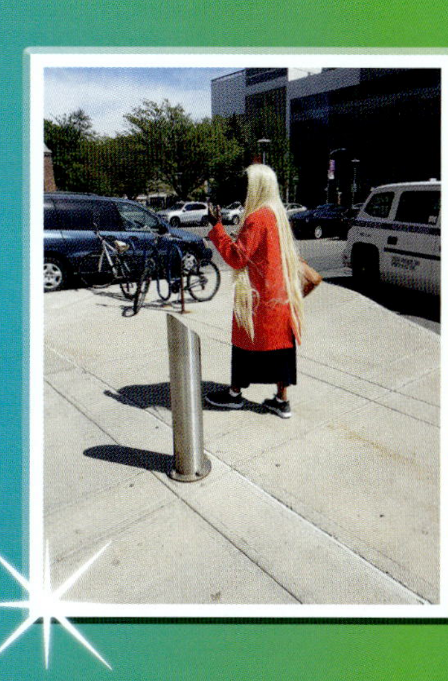
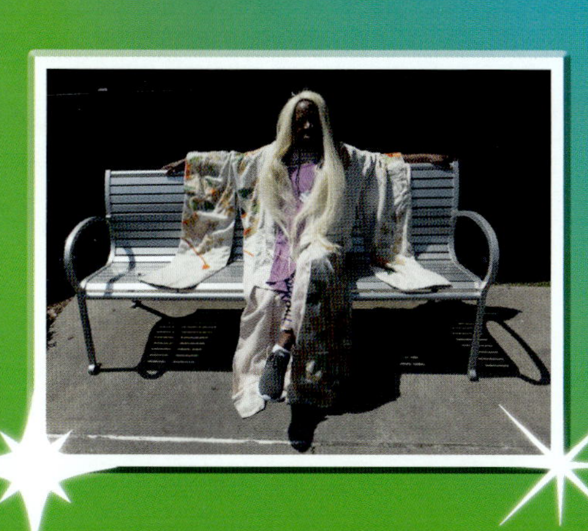
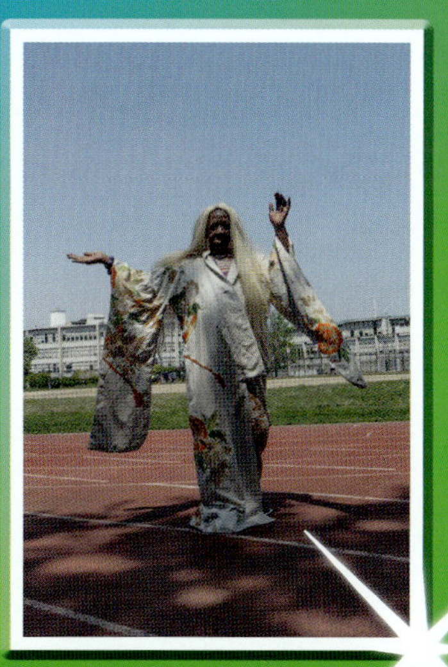

THE LOVER

CHA'VES JAMALL

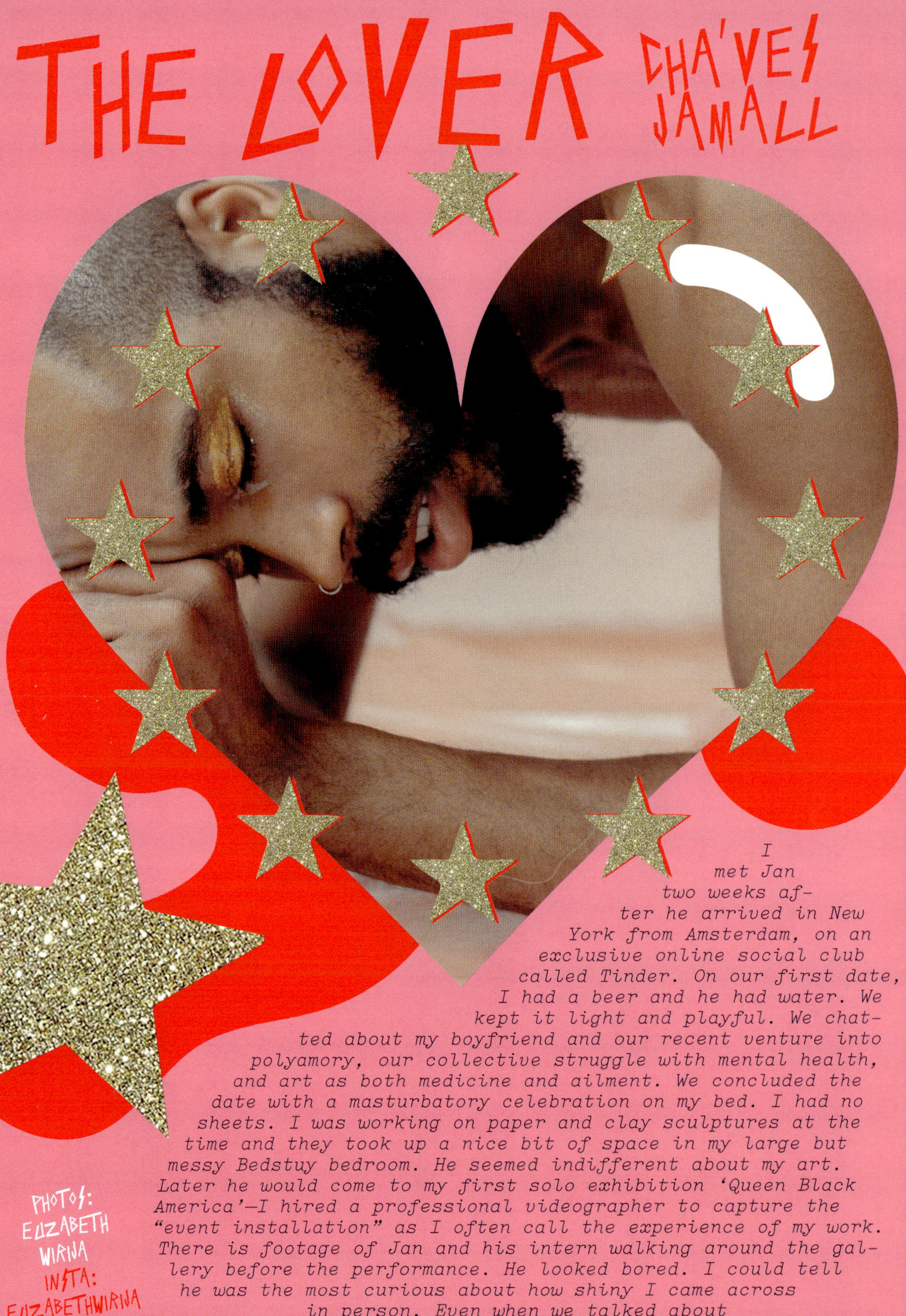

I met Jan two weeks after he arrived in New York from Amsterdam, on an exclusive online social club called Tinder. On our first date, I had a beer and he had water. We kept it light and playful. We chatted about my boyfriend and our recent venture into polyamory, our collective struggle with mental health, and art as both medicine and ailment. We concluded the date with a masturbatory celebration on my bed. I had no sheets. I was working on paper and clay sculptures at the time and they took up a nice bit of space in my large but messy Bedstuy bedroom. He seemed indifferent about my art. Later he would come to my first solo exhibition 'Queen Black America'—I hired a professional videographer to capture the "event installation" as I often call the experience of my work. There is footage of Jan and his intern walking around the gallery before the performance. He looked bored. I could tell he was the most curious about how shiny I came across in person. Even when we talked about

PHOTOS: ELIZABETH WIRIJA
INSTA: ELIZABETHWIRIJA

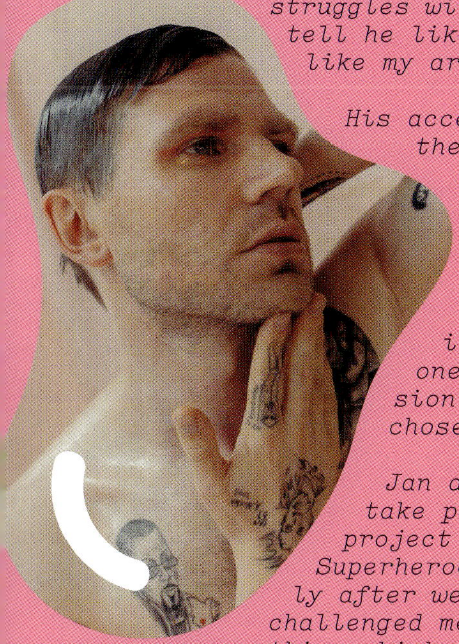

my struggles with depression and romantic codependency, I could tell he liked the way I packaged my trauma. I guess he did like my art.

His accent didn't bother me. In fact, looking back at the second half of my twenties I seem to have exclusively dated white non-Americans. Most notably a tall ginger called Lachlan who moved to New York from Australia to be with me. And after him, Bertrand, an easy-going Frenchman I moved to Paris for to be with. I still feel bad for leaving Bertrand in France. It's the only time in my dating career that I was the one who made the decision to leave. I chose art.

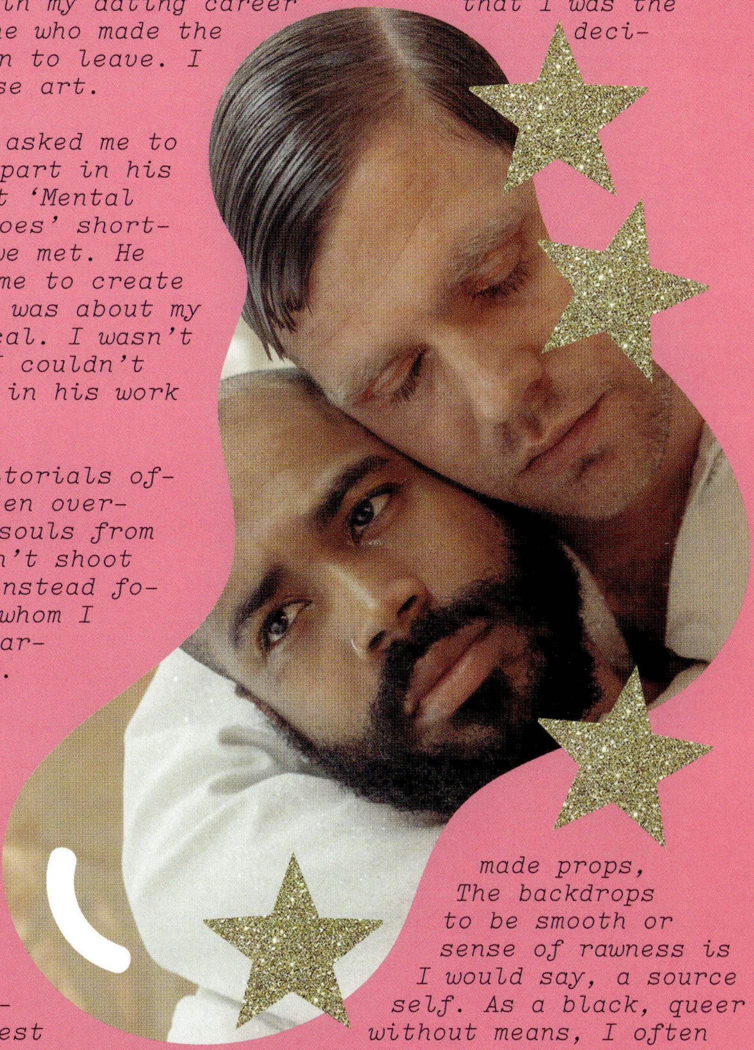

Jan asked me to take part in his project 'Mental Superheroes' shortly after we met. He challenged me to create something which was about my experience. I was skeptical. I wasn't sure if I liked his work. I couldn't tell if he was being honest in his work or exploitative.

is portraits and fashion editorials often feature those who have been overooked; weary and rebellious souls from l over the world. Jan doesn't shoot e culturally favorable but instead foses his eye on sex workers (whom I ke to call emotional humanitarns), the poor and minorities. en I look at his photos they mind me of what I would have cked to wear in kindergarn if I had been allowed to ess myself. His work is a llage of colors and mixed tterns, seemingly handmade props, d crudely hung backdrops. The backdrops eem to have no ambition to be smooth or rinkle-free, in fact, a sense of rawness is elcomed. This "rawness" is, I would say, a source f tension between Jan and myself. As a black, queer erson growing up in the Midwest without means, I often ind myself seeking to elevate brown and black bodies in my creative work. levate them in ways that show them as celestial beings, shiny and bright, trong bodies that shimmer with perfection. While this seems like a fantasy, believe that this is who we are, that this is who we've been. When I look pecifically about the conversation of global blackness—we have been stolen rom. Culture has been stolen from us. From music to fashion to "urban" vernacular. Things that we create are often taken from us and called something else. As a farmer of the village, as a creator, I have grown fatigued. I reject narratives brought to us by white culture that show us as less than. That show us as a flimsy caricature of ourselves. That show us unkept, without dimension or refinement. For this reason, I didn't allow Jan

to capture my image but enlisted instead the help of a female artist of color. It's not that I don't believe that Jan's work doesn't provide nuance, texture, and honesty. It's just that I'm unsure if the way that he is presenting the story is harmful to the global narrative.

Art is about questions. I believe that true queerness is having messy conversations.

We all live in different corners of the room, animating life with the moon and the sun shining on us all in unique ways.
I appreciate the friction that my relationship with Jan brings to my life. I appreciate the openness that every contributor to this zine has brought to the project.

Jan: That felt like an abrupt ending. Can you talk more about your mental health?

I'm an extrovert who struggles with depression and anxiety. I am concerned that my persona keeps me from true closeness, with myself and lovers. I am currently battling codependency. I worry that having to productize my trauma will leave me empty.

I'm fatigued.
New York is killing me.
I miss my family.

The only thing keeping me alive is my core belief that 'I Can'. A voice told me at a young age that I could be great. I believed it.

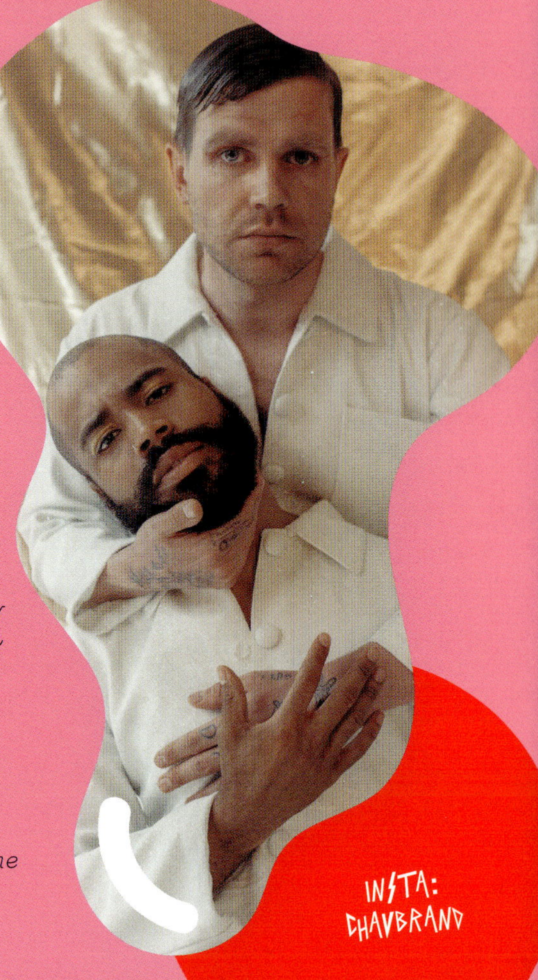

INSTA:
CHAVBRAND

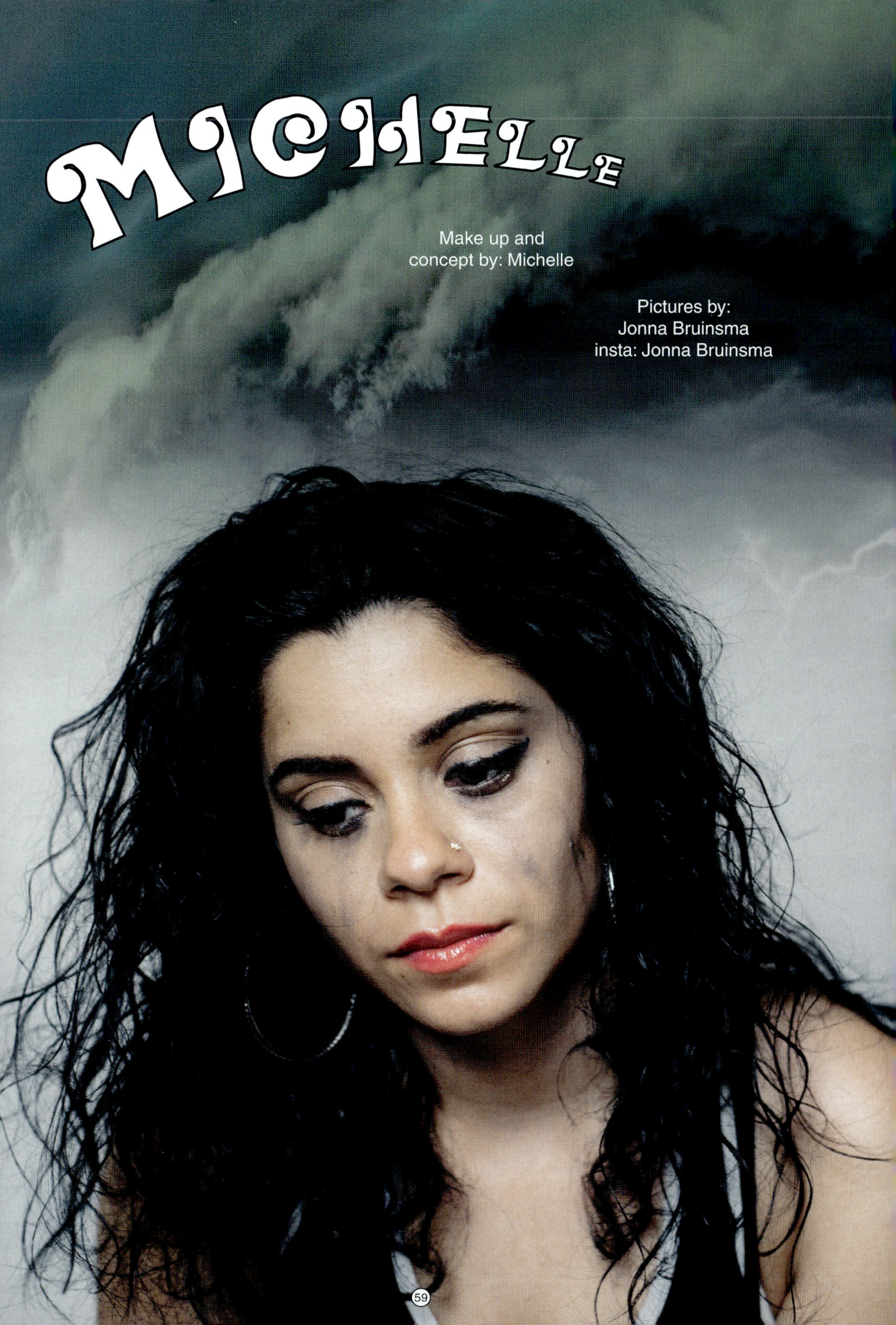
MICHELLE
Make up and
concept by: Michelle
Pictures by:
Jonna Bruinsma
insta: Jonna Bruinsma

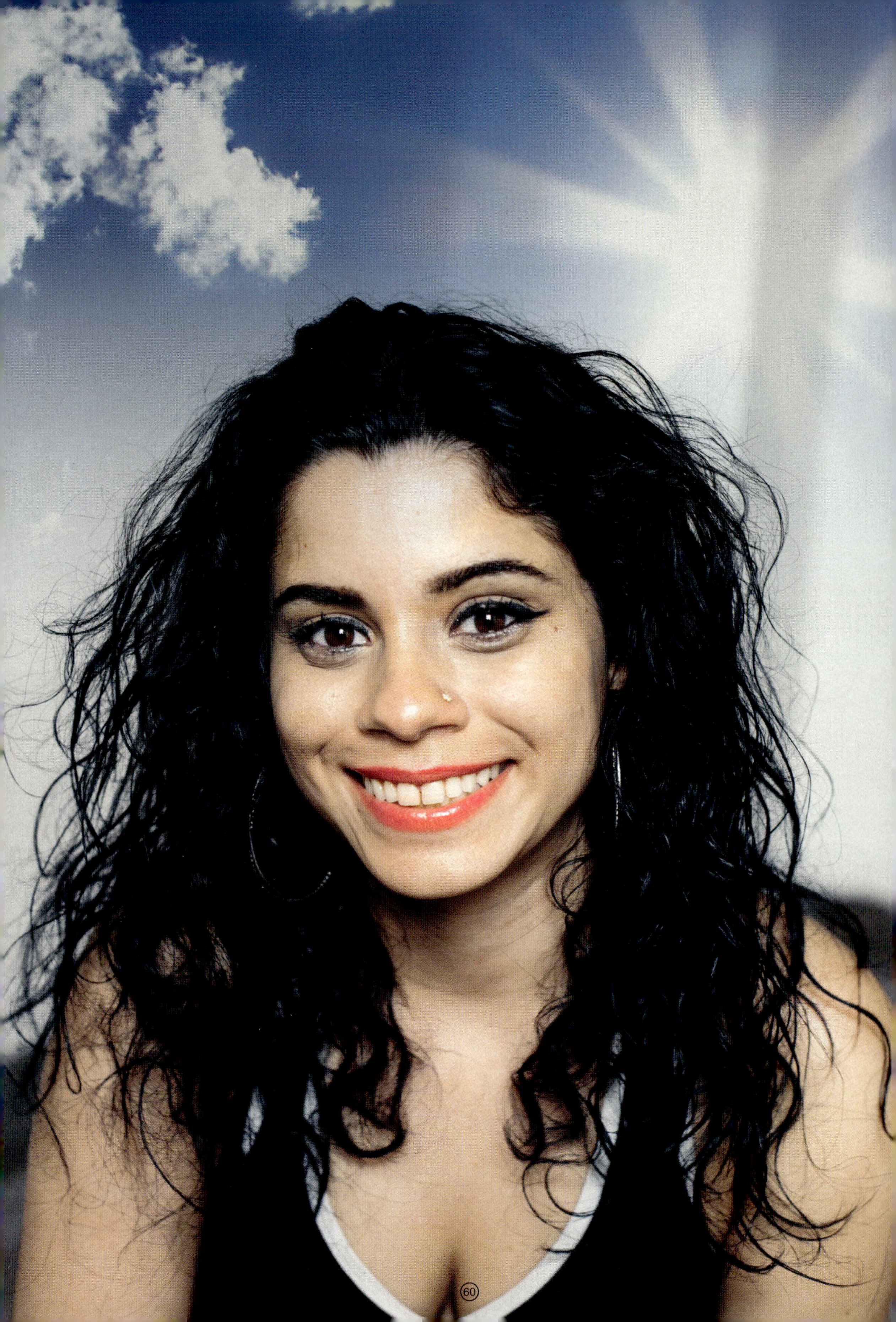

MATEUS, THE YOUNG PHOTOGRAPHER I ADMIRE

In New York I met Mateus, a photographer I already knew from Instagram and who I really admired.

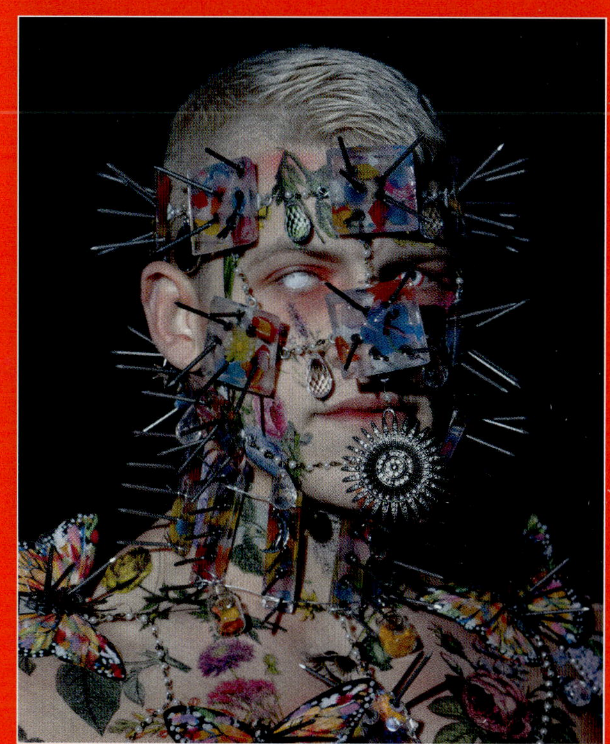

AUSTIN insta: @emptypools

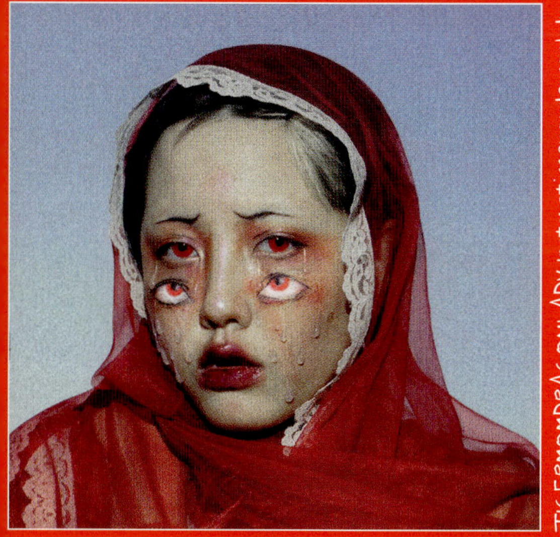

TIGERMOMDRAGONLADY insta:@tigermomdragonlady

I found out that he romanticizes pain and suffering in the same way I romanticize "craziness".

He told me that when he was five years old, he was sitting in a car in Oklahoma with his mom, sister and brother when a man walked out of the bushes and into the middle of the road. He had been shot, so he was covered in blood, and he walked towards their car.

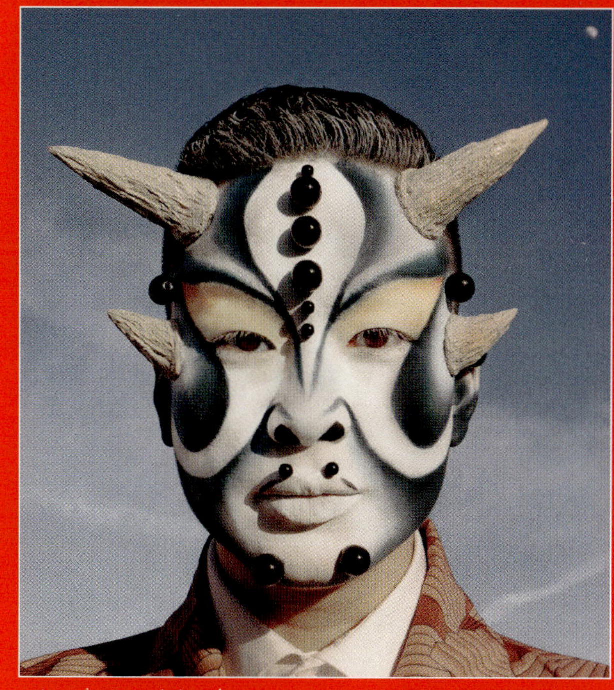

YUNI insta: @babyuni_

Everybody was shocked, Mateus as well, but somehow he also saw a kind of beauty in it.

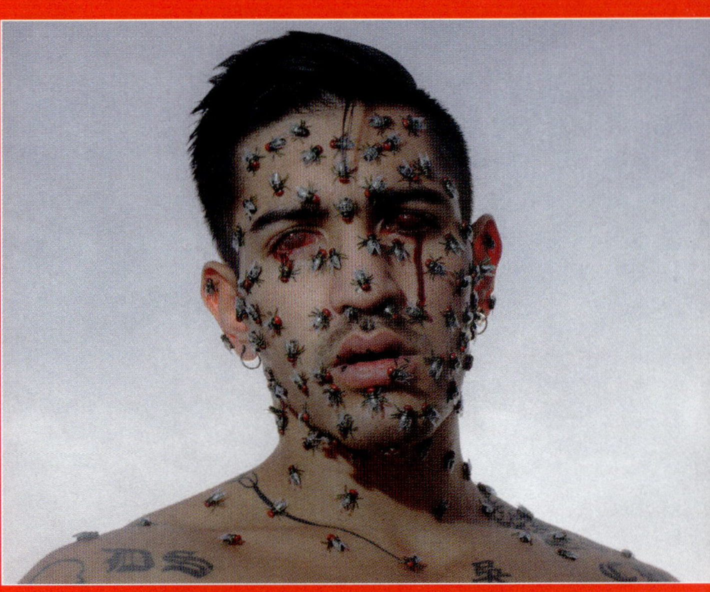

FORREST insta: @4stwu

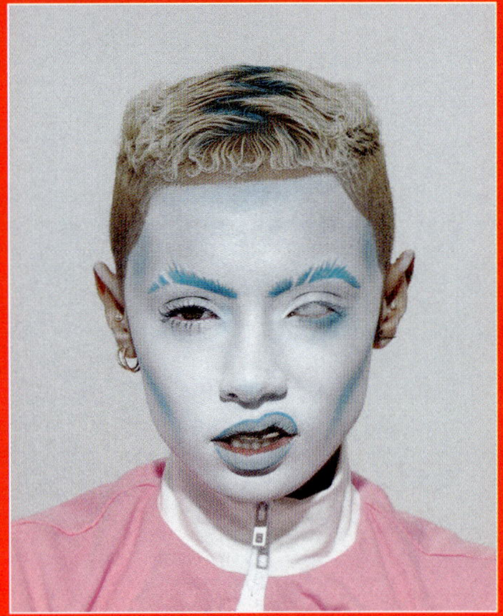

JAZZELLE insta: @uglyworldwide

Ever since this experience he has always been attracted to pain, darkness and suffering. To find power in those things he also had to cope with a lot of other things that were going on in his life.

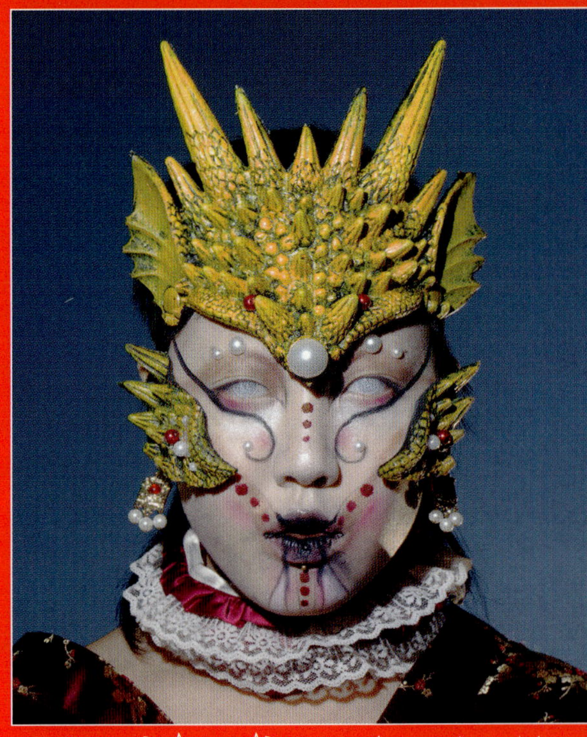

TIGERMOMDRAGONLADY Insta:@tigermomdragonlady

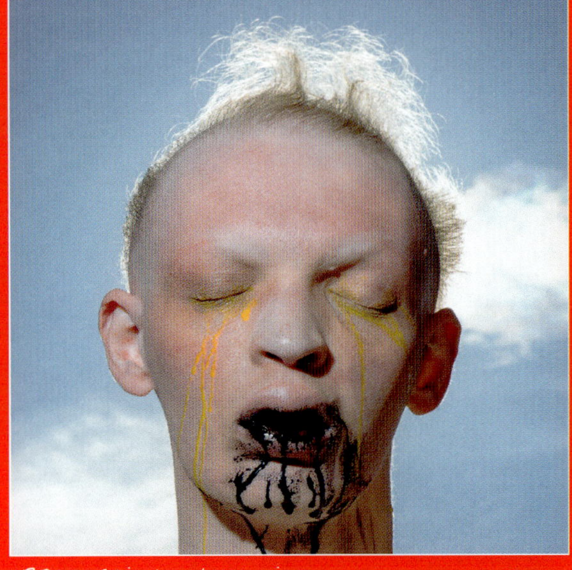

BROOKSY insta: @brooksginan

But as with a nasty magic spell it turned out that this thing also worked the other way around: he didn't only see beauty in pain, but pain appeared to be in all beauty as well.

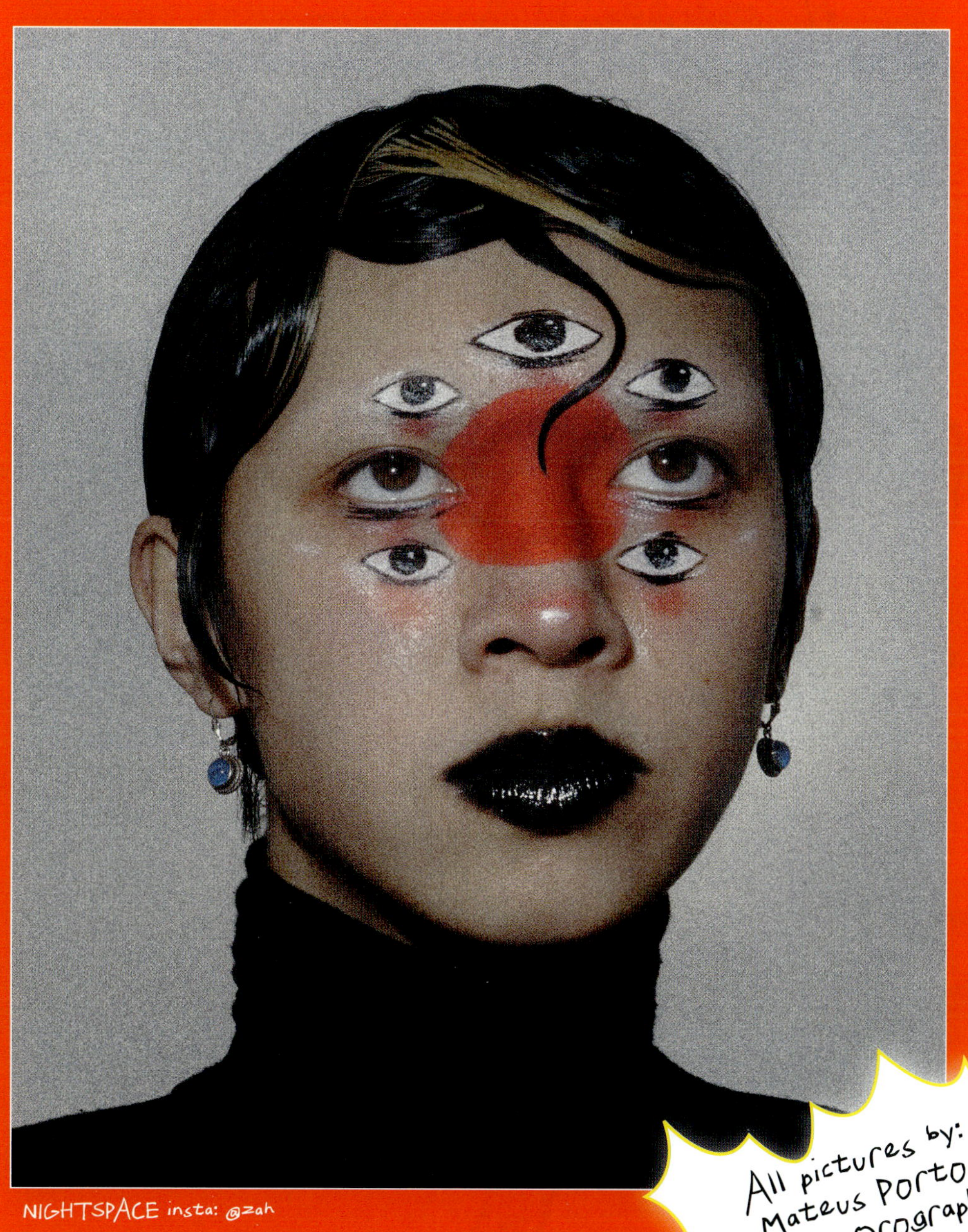

NIGHTSPACE insta: @zah

All pictures by:
Mateus Porto
(insta: Orograph)

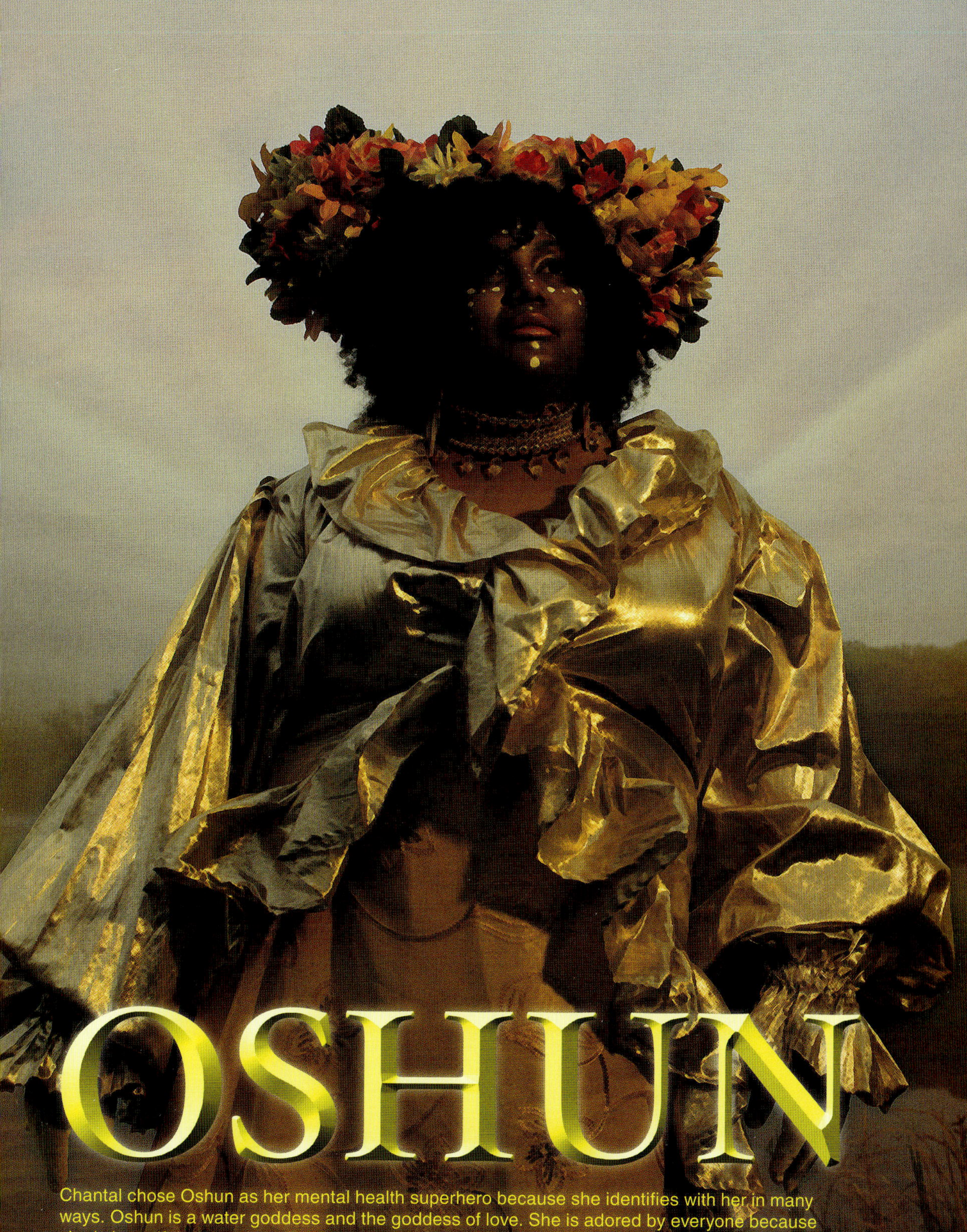

OSHUN

Chantal chose Oshun as her mental health superhero because she identifies with her in many ways. Oshun is a water goddess and the goddess of love. She is adored by everyone because she is beautiful and caring. She gives so much to others and is always smiling, which is why nobody sees that she is dying on the inside.

Black Woman!

Do you find me beautiful?

Black Woman!
Skin like cocoa beans, shiny and glistening as the sun
Arises its sweetest scent
And aromatic sensuality
Chocolates of different shades,
Nevertheless you crave that immortal flavour.

Do you find me beautiful?

Black Woman!
Pride as majestic as her supple breasts
Slaps, Scars
Battered, Bruised
But those glorious hips
That stubborn strut,
Refuse the hand of evil, malice,
That inherently beguile her.

Do you find me beautiful?
Black Woman!
Hair as strong as our foremothers' backs,
Pressing, Burning, Ironing, Whipping, Cut-down
Damaged.
Maybe eventually.
But grows out stronger
Like future generations she bears in her loins.

Do you find me beautiful?
Black Woman!
Whips, Cotton bales,
Humiliation, Hatred,
Raped, Pulverised
Stolen dignity.
Challenging
Of all her mothers combined.

Do you find me beautiful?
Black Woman!
Succulent lips, Broad noses
Image of God.

Look in the mirror!
Those fearless eyes,
Challenging
Life's irreverent stares.

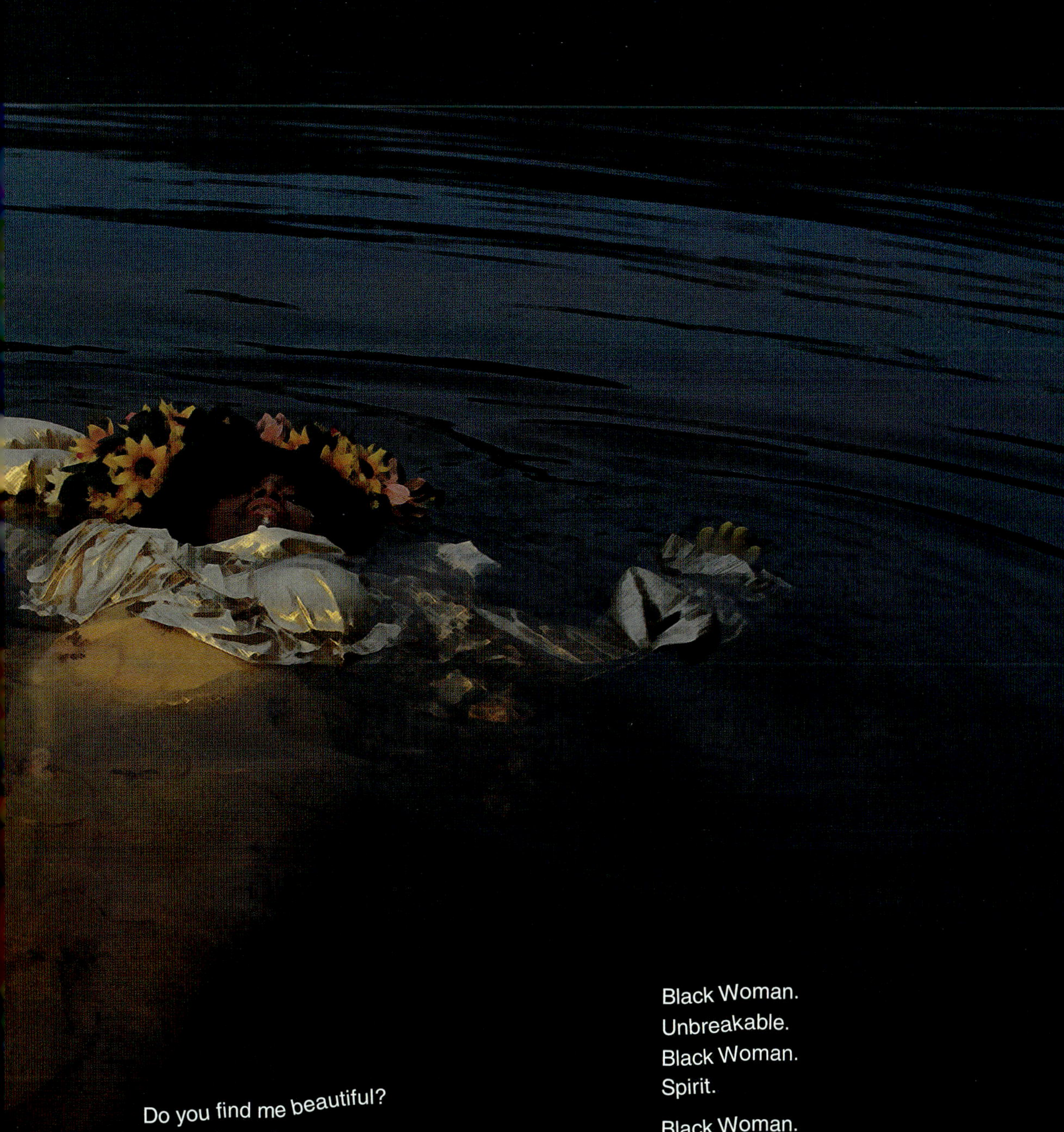

Do you find me beautiful?
Black Woman!
Succulent lips, Broad noses
Image of God.

Look in the mirror!
Those fearless eyes,
Challenging
Life's irreverent stares.

Black Woman.
Unbreakable.
Black Woman.
Spirit.

Black Woman.
Pulchritudinous.
Black Woman!
Black Woman.

text and starring: Chantal J Antoine
Styling: Devon Alonzo Savage
insta: devonalonzosavage
Photography Assistant: Jonna Bruinsma
(insta: Jonna Bruinsma)

SIMONE VAN SAARLOOS – CALL ME CRAZY IF YOU WANT

I met Simone in a bar in New York, around the corner from the hospital. In Amsterdam she's viewed as a brilliant thinker and one of the most prominent young philosophers. Talking with her she'll shift topics from a Persian poet to something she saw in a laundromat to a feminist freedom fighter. Sometimes, when I ask her for practical advice she'll tell me "I can only respond to this with a lesbian poem", which she'll look up on her phone right then and there. All things which I would find annoying if it was anyone else, but with Simone I think it's charming. At the same time, the way she talks "a stream of incredibly diverse associations which are freely weaved together" reminds me of how some people in the psychiatric hospital talk. But it causes the people in the hospital to be branded as "crazy" while Simone is called "brilliant". I asked her to write a text about this.

Episode
Embodying a category
IF I CELEBRATE YOU CALLING ME BRILLIANT, AM I CRAZY TOO?

When I got Jan's voicemail, I listened to it like I always do: while doing several things at the same time. Thus, I have a sensuous memory of when I heard his explanation and quest for this comic book. I was doing the dishes and scrubbing a sauce pan with an exaggerated amount of strength, squashing the hairs of the brush until the plastic of the head was beat-scrubbing the pan. I like to flex my muscles while doing housework. Someone once saw me trenching the floor with a vacuum cleaner and thought I carried a lot of anger. I believe my surroundings are just too soft to equal what is inside me (this is a sign of privilege).

While Jan talked from my phone, I could see his hands moving along with his words. He continuously twists and unfolds his hands while talking, a tide of gestures, turning his tattoos outwards, showing 'Dada'. He said "It may sound a bit strange, but I consider you brilliant, but also crazy, because of the associative way you think." He mentioned a lesbian poem I had referred to while talking about something very non-lesbian and non-poetic twice. It sounded like the lesbian poem proved to him that I was brilliant. He felt a little hesitant, he said, calling me crazy. He didn't want to offend me.

Actually, I felt complimented to the max. If I have been called brilliant before, then only in a celebrating outcry. Jan contrasted brilliance with crazy and it thereby became a judgement that sounded quite trustworthy.

I also saw it as a compliment because of my white logic. As Leslie Jamison describes in *The Recovering. Intoxication and Aftermath*, brilliance, living a genius life, is a well-guarded title. Basically, you need to be white and male. Preferably, this white man drinks heavily because his mind becomes more lucid and true when he does so. Often, the genius will also have many romantic and sexual escapades that mean little to him emotionally, but are still necessary to support his genius. White logic refers to the fact that a black man drinking is a problem while a white man drinking can be a genius–his drinking doesn't annihilate his dignity, it even adds to his status. Jamison describes how women are excluded from this logic: drinking women are a problem too. Crazy white men can be brilliant; crazy white women are hysterical (and certainly bad mothers).

I, however, embraced the "crazy" Jan reserved for me. From my privileged position as a middle-class, educated, young white woman, the adjective "crazy" could improve my image, my seriousness as an artist.

So the crazy-stigma wasn't much of a problem. Next was "brilliant". This had to sit with me for a while before I realized I've never experienced myself as intelligent. I do have the conventional story about teachers expecting very little of me, advising a lower level of high school education than my test results indicated, and diagnosing my desire for more-more (self-sedated with weed) as "out of control". I went through a series of psychological test to see if I might be extraordinarily developed, and therefore bored, and therefore unruly and refusing. They didn't find a clear-cut answer and that, in and of itself, was problematic. The bouquets of red cuts on my arms and legs were explained as gender-trouble, or attributed to the neighbor's cat's claws. I remember coming into the ER as a ten year old with a burst appendix and the doctors asking me over and over if I might be pregnant. When I told him this wasn't possible, he suggested that maybe something had happened to me against my will and that maybe I was pregnant. At that moment, saying something had happened, would have been dangerous in a new way: looking for the wrong cause (pregnancy) while I needed urgent care. I learned that pain needs to translate into a scar or an illness in order to evoke interest. Questions arose when quick solutions were wanted.

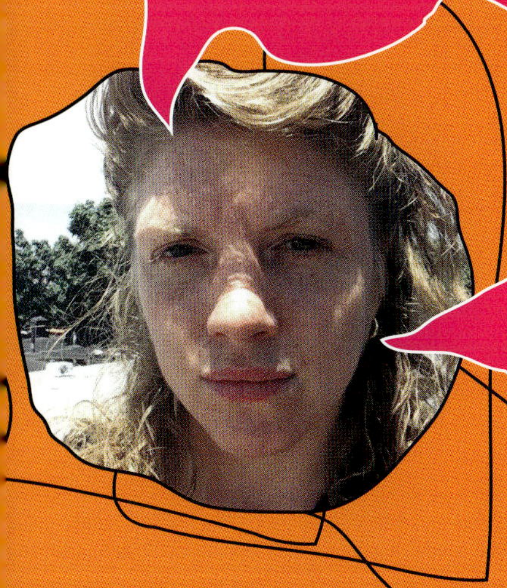

I longed for questions with insoluble problems. Thus, I went to study philosophy, finished my bachelor cum laude, but still never thought of myself as smart. That is not self-deprecating. It comes from a deep distrust of all the language and structures invented to test and measure us.

"Difficult" was the adjective which I was generally awarded. Writing makes difficult really quite bearable. Difficult on paper is a different kind of difficult. It is not of the "I am" kind, but of the "we share" kind.

Episode Meet the Goddess SOMEONE ASKED ME WHY I CONTINUOUSLY SAY "SORRY"

"You apologize for every breath you take, even though you are such a feminist."

I tend to turn this someone's reasoning around: as a woman in this world, I've learned to apologize for being present, and thus I became a feminist. There is a direct correlation between my growing interest in feminism and the surplus of apologies I express daily. But feminism isn't at stake here. The true ontology of the "sorry" lies elsewhere. My continuous apologies are meant for God. I don't believe in God but I tend to feel the world is inhabited by Goddesses. As I don't believe in God as a(n) (authoritative) figure, I see the Goddesses as an extension of myself.

You might call me crazy when I say the world is filled with God-extensions of myself. Walt Whitman wrote "I am large, I contain multitudes". This phrase (among others) made him an eternally celebrated genius. The trick is not to say the right thing, but to say the whatever-thing at the right time. As what can become the "right thing" to say needs to come from the right body–a body who's voice is heard as a human's voice and not as an animal outcry.

When I say sorry, it isn't because I expect another person–the person or people present to hear my apology–to condemn me. I honestly expect the other person to think nice things (this may be cruel optimism). The apology is meant for the broader, extended, elaborate, transcending version of myself; the one that reaches beyond my perceivable skin. It is the me that creeps into the floor, that shapes the crooked window sill and the wall and the wallpaper's curled edges near the ceiling, the dust in the air, the hair above your lip. It is the spilled me that I sometimes strongly perceive but often only acknowledge theoretically. It is the me that doesn't accept designed restrictions, that doesn't acknowledge subject-object relations, that fights against separation and categories and enclosing lines–whether boxes or circles. With every move I make and every word I utter, I experience the loss of possibilities not taken advantage of, simply by engaging in one particular movement or choice of wording. My sorry tries to acknowledge that loss. My sorries are an acknowledgment of all that the goddesses experience and know of, while I, a human body with limited limbs and senses, only inhabit a minimal part of the possible.

Episode Keeping my mouth shut AFRAID OF SPILLING EVERYWHERE

I had a blackout on stage. An audience of five hundred people stared at me. I wore glitter shoes to support-shine my talk, but nothing came out of my mouth. There was a camera recording my performance for TV. Backstage there was a production company I fiercely disagreed with. They had organized a day full of talks by philosophers, twelve speakers of which only two were women, and one was a man of color. We were asked to speak about our favorite philosopher. My colleagues chose Plato, Kant and Heidegger. The world may be round but our knowledge is still flat–the limit of our own horizon perceived as the end.

I chose Rachel Carson, the American biologist who fought against the use of hazardous pesticides. Carson died of cancer in 1964, but didn't tell anyone about her disease: she feared her colleagues would view her as a "weak, sickly female". I talked about Carson precisely because I had, before then, never read her work and hadn't known her name. I argued that making an unknown your favorite is something we should strive for, so that we don't reproduce the same names and scientists and philosophers over and over again. Carson's unlimited interest in deep sea life and her romantic correspondence with a woman encouraged me to talk about the queer ways of living that can be found under the water's surface. Studying life in the deep sea can open our traditional binary thinking into a more fluid, interconnected vision. I mentioned Astrida Neimanis' flow-stimulating article on "Hydrofeminism", in which she argues that thinking from a "water-perspective" allows us to think differently about responsibility: infants in the Arctic fall ill because their mother's milk is polluted due to industrial water use. When thinking from a water-perspective, boundaries and borders start to matter less.

Thinking about how the camera needed one straight story (and not a stumbling story that started slowly, which can be perfectly charming with a live audience only) I decided that I would start over, walked off stage and returned immediately, afraid I would not dare to go back if I allowed myself to pause in the dark. The audience applauded gently and I preached what I had prepared.

I chose Rachel Carson and was very convinced of the importance of her story. But I was unable to tell it. I just stared at the five hundred people looking up at me. Behind me, visuals of deep sea life gave the impression that this talk was moving along awesomely.

By then, what I had prepared beforehand was no longer what I wanted to say. What I needed to do, what I should have done, was to sit down on the edge of the large stage, get closer to the audience, and explain to them the great pain I carried in my legs and chest and head due to this day, which was presented to them as a kind of intellectual entertainment. I would let my legs dangle so that my glitter shoes would disco ball the theater and I would tell them how it felt impossible to speak, because here I was, one out of two women in a twelve person lineup, after many debates with the organization about what "doing better" actually means.

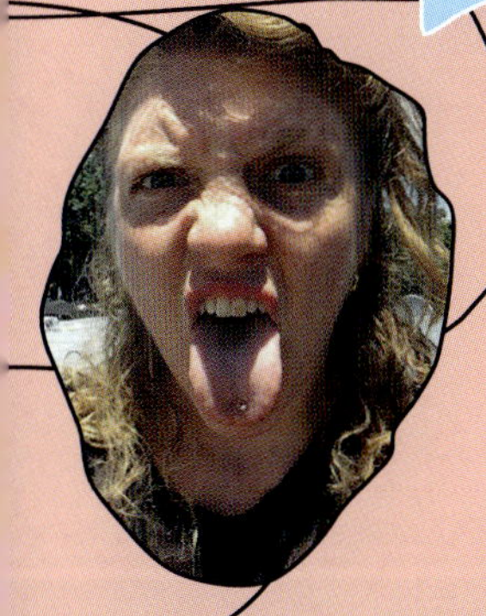

Just before I went up on stage I encountered my colleagues who shrug-shook my hand, ready to do their usual gig with their usual talk about the usual Plato, Kant and Heidegger; talks that do not seem to excite any new ideas or challenge the old ones, but do not bore anyone either.

I would tell the audience about the hours of conversation I had with the organization. Not just about the lineup, but also about my own talk, as they wondered if it was truly necessary to make a connection between Carson's struggle as a scientist and current troubles as a female philosopher (or female anything). I wanted to tell the audience that they had paid for fairly expensive tickets but that I was not getting paid for all this extra work. The fee I was promised may have been just enough, had I only been busy preparing the talk, but it definitely wasn't enough taking into account the labor that goes into explaining and convincing a self-assured organization about the inequalities they reproduce. Explaining and convincing, while trying to remain nice. Not trying, just: while remaining nice. While remaining nice because, even though you don't get paid well, you also need the money, which is not enough. While remaining nice because you have to believe in these people's desire to change, because they say they love philosophy and the audience they cater to loves philosophy and you love philosophy. Though you know love means many different things, you don't want to be lonely in loving and thus you try sharing. You remain nice and try till the niceness and the trying has depleted you and everything you tried to protect by being nice now only exists in remembrance.

I should have sat down at the edge but didn't. From that day onward, I quit speaking. I still showed up on stages and still said yes to talk shows and TV, but I stopped giving my presence.

After a while though, the blackout started to untangle into different threads and layers: the cameras for the TV show, the audience staring, the heartfelt tribute to Rachel Carson, my sadness about the almost all-male list of speakers and the almost all-white lineup, the dialectic between I shouldn't be here and someone has to say this, feeling like a trick pony, a window dressing prop welcomed to convey the rebellious message of "this shouldn't be like this!", and the organizers and curators with their eternal "go slow!" response.

When the layers became visible, I realized that this layered structure was usually what allowed me to speak out loud, instead of barricading me. Most of the time, when I do feel free speaking publicly, I tumble and fall while also being carried. A deep kind of being carried can only be reached when falling rather far. I move while being pulled and pushed by different tides and currents. While speaking, I often experience a large amount of thoughts and connotations that I need to push away in order to remain clear enough to be understood.

After a while though, the blackout started to untangle into different threads and layers: the cameras for the TV show, the audience staring, the heartfelt tribute to Rachel Carson, my sadness about the almost all-male list of speakers and the almost all-white lineup, the dialectic between I shouldn't be here and someone has to say this, feeling like a trick pony, a window dressing prop welcomed to convey the rebellious message of "this shouldn't be like this!", and the organizers and curators with their eternal "go slow!" response.

Every word in a sentence leads to new thoughts, images and feelings. Sometimes, in a public interview or panel setting, I cannot hear the question, because every single word and bit of syntax becomes a question itself. And it is not just the words. Tone is present, lighting, gesture, a sound elsewhere in the room, the wire connecting the speaker with an invisible controller backstage–everything is part of this tentacled reality. Everything fights to be its present everything–the hair above your lip may not be meaningful in our conversation about budget cuts, but it is fucking present anyway.

Most people seem to ignore those particles as unnecessary details. I've attuned and adapted and try to compress the huge amount of incentives. But some of these lines, I do not push away, I let them ramble into expression, try to vocalize them coherently. Sometimes these curvy thoughts and spontaneous side paths are greatly appreciated. Other times they're not. I try not to be afraid of raised eyebrows and puzzled looks. I know that I need to remain somewhat open to this drifting or else all thought will evaporate, like when I tried to ignore all the layers of influence in order to do my talk about Rachel Carson, resulting in complete silence.

I don't see this layered structure, this tumbling experience, as a distraction. The more I concentrate, the more the maze/the sea/the fullness expands. People might tell me "Don't get distracted from the main topic, from the central question", but I wonder: do they know what the topic, the question really is? Don't they feel that by defining the, they miss an amazing amount of other aspects, questions, associations, senses, realities, anecdotes?

In quickly suppressing some lines of thought thereby committing to a sense of clarity which is usually encouraged–I'm supported by the goddesses. The goddesses I trust in keeping, treasuring and witnessing the maze/the sea/the fullness. I can temporarily ignore certain lines of thought, because I know the goddesses watch the lines of thought. By witnessing, they acknowledge the realness of the maze, the importance of the sea and empower the fullness. They allow me to neglect and betray the presence of the maze, sea, fullness.

On the day of the blackout, the layered structure of reality became clogged. I could not feel the goddesses telling me "Issa okay, you may dig into one line of reality, speak out loud, follow the question posed for the sake of clarity, it's A-Okay, ignoring what else is present, because we are here, witnessing the complexity of reality."

Any
fool can get
into an ocean
But it takes a Goddess
To get out of one.
What's true of oceans is true, of course,
Of labyrinths and poems. When you start swimming
Through riptide of rhythms and the metaphor's seaweed
You need to be a good swimmer or a born Goddess
To get back out of them
– Jack Spicer

Episode You'd not be crazy in a crazy world

Crazy is the opposite of control. Crazy is the opposite of regulation. Imagine a world in which crazy doesn't exist, because it doesn't oppose axnything.

Episode When crazy is all around you, making you crazy

You have moved to a country in which people speak another language. In which the people smile when they say something rude. In which yes means no or later means never. You think everything is weird but are constantly told you are weird. If you adapt too much no one will tell you how they do it here. Only if you claim your "weirdness", proudly wear a "Good Immigrant" sticker, will people start demonstrating the most simple, daily things, will people start explaining normal as a lesson instead of just subtly living it.

A young man from Russia tells me how he learned about "having boundaries" after moving to The Netherlands. This, he says, meant nothing in the country where he was born and raised. Having boundaries made no sense, because the state can always interfere in your personal life. Your personal life is subject to the state's commands and wishes.

I ask him how you learn to have boundaries. He tells me that it started with crossing other people's boundaries, then being told he was crossing them. He would offer someone half of his lunch and they would say "no" and he would say "yes, you are having it". Not respecting boundaries can be confused with being nice. "I thought 'I want this from you and thus I make you do it, and then the same the other way around: you can tell me what you want me to do. It is a mutual trade of force. You can use me and I'll use you.' " Tapping into the needs and desires of another person wasn't something he knew how to do naturally, but as an immigrant he developed it.

He says Dutch people are great at boundaries, "also in sex." He was happy to learn that Dutch women don't do what they don't want to do. "They seem to know what they want– and what they don't want."

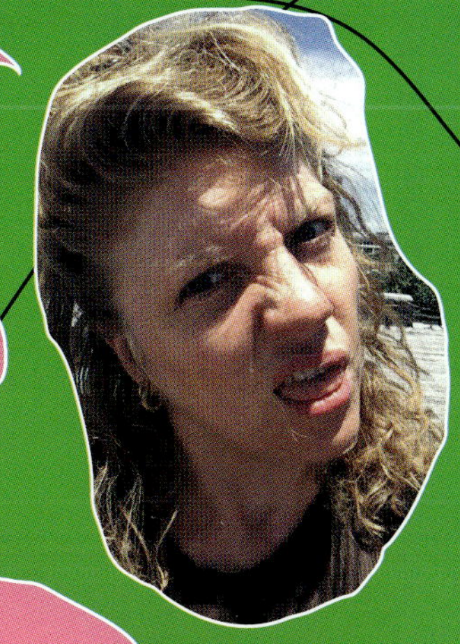

I wonder whether it is some kind of shame that makes me nod and agree with his impressions, and then pretend that boundaries were a big thing in my youth. I've never felt someone crossed my boundaries, but from a societal stance –from the discourse that is available to understand what is normal and healthy–I can say that people have crossed boundaries, I just don't necessarily recognize them as mine. I don't identify with having boundaries, because I feel nothing truly belongs to me. Boundaries are someone else's designed and designated space. Now that someone, evaluating Dutch culture from an "Outsider Perspective", tells me about boundaries, I worry that I have missed some cultural reality. Maybe that is exactly what sums up the Dutch cultural narrative: one is made to feel as if a certain standard is clear and present for everyone except for you. You come to think that others share a publicly known truth, while you are personally failing. Hello liberal thinking! Society is well-arranged; you just aren't picking the fruits because you fail to reach for them.

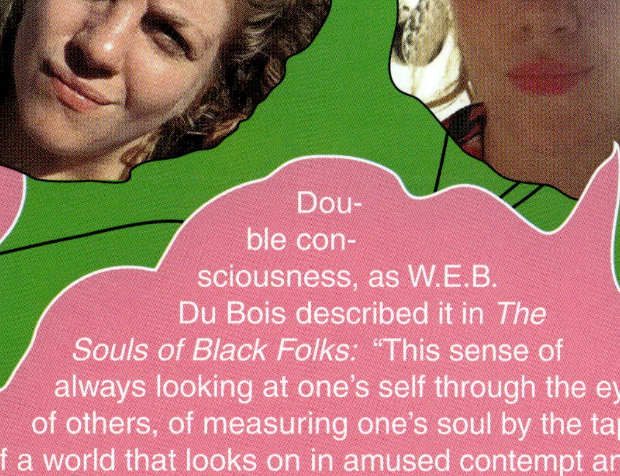

Doublethink, as George Orwell described it in 1984: "The act of holding, simultaneously, two opposite, individually exclusive ideas or opinions and believing in both simultaneously and absolutely. Doublethink requires using logic against logic or suspending disbelief in the contradiction."

Double consciousness, as W.E.B. Du Bois described it in *The Souls of Black Folks:* "This sense of always looking at one's self through the eyes of others, of measuring one's soul by the tape of a world that looks on in amused contempt and pity. One ever feels his two-ness,—an American, a Negro; two souls, two thoughts, two unreconciled strivings; two warring ideals in one dark body, whose dogged strength alone keeps it from being torn asunder."

Can a very concrete kind of weird–being bicultural comfort the mind, as the in-between position–of being an acknowledged outsider–can make palpable what is felt inside already?

Episode Why no one feels love around me, and other proofs of brilliance

What does the love of a brilliant person look like? My friend Romana Vrede talks about her autistic son, Charlie, who embodies sixteen years of age but cannot talk and go to school like most teenagers do. He knows some sign language. He utters sounds of which no one knows what they mean exactly.

Charlie is an artist, says Romana. When people see him as an artist and not as an autist, he becomes a different person; his “problems” may suddenly become talents. “Charlie experiences everything at once and everything is equally important to him. There is no hierarchy of information.” Romana acknowledges she is interpreting, but then, Charlie knows her, like, he really knows her. So she must know something too. “To him, everything is big and nothing is big. Everything is present and thus everything is a lot and everything is nothing.” When Romana talks about Charlie’s ontology, I recognize his (or her interpretation of his) experience.

As his mother, she has to assure herself of his love. She has to know, but she cannot verify it in the usual ways. “I have never talked to someone for sixteen years without getting a clear response you may call that some serious love practice.”

I want to take her explanation of her son and throw the sentences around me like confetti, celebrating what usually seems like a burden. Especially to those I try to love. I’m idealistically non-monogamous; that is not the problem. In polyamorous structures too, people like to feel special. And I do consider my lovers very special. But I consider everyone very special. Everything is a lot and everything is nothing. My kisses are focused in the moment but they are not a hierarchical evaluation. They never signify an “I have chosen you over another”.

We call Charlie an artist. We call him brilliant. Whenever I think of brilliant people and love, I think of the structures that allow someone to flourish: the structures of care–structures of getting a meal in time and structures of not getting in the way (loud vacuum cleaning while big thoughts are thought). When I think of brilliant people and love, I remind myself that the Rodin-image of a thinker would look different if he was a pregnant woman with an eight month belly. When I think of the brilliant works that have survived, I think of the forgotten enslaved who have fed, washed and carried the thinker, the enslaved who drew and calculated what the “master” would later claim to be his own. I think of the female artist, Elsa von Freytag-Loringhoven, who made Duchamp’s famous urinoir without ever getting credited. In the proximity of something outstanding–something celebrated as special–everything becomes suspicious. When we consider everything to be outstanding (brilliant and crazy), will exploitation become less prevalent?

INSTA: SVSAARLOOS

THE INTERN

OH GOD,
I AM JANS INTERN AND FIRST HE BROUGHT ME TO THIS PSYCHIATRIC HOSPITAL, AND NOW HE WANTS ME TO PARTICIPATE IN THIS COMIC AS WELL.
BUT I'M AFRAID I'M JUST NOT CRAZY ENOUGH TO DO THAT

I'D RATHER JUST ENJOY THE SUN.

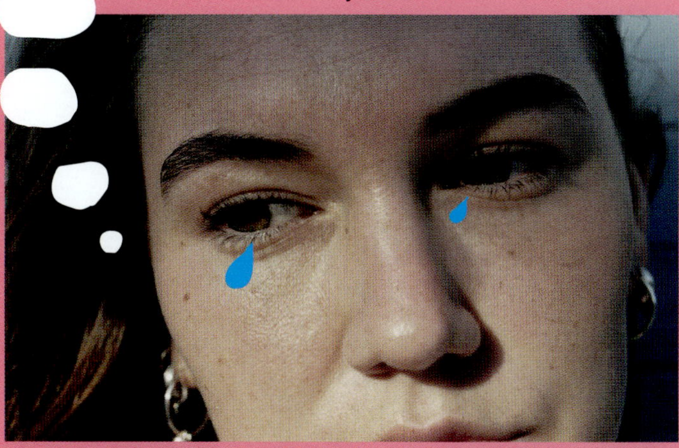

PICTURE AND TEXT: JONNA BRUINSMA INSTA: JONNA BRUINSMA

THE BEST FRIEND

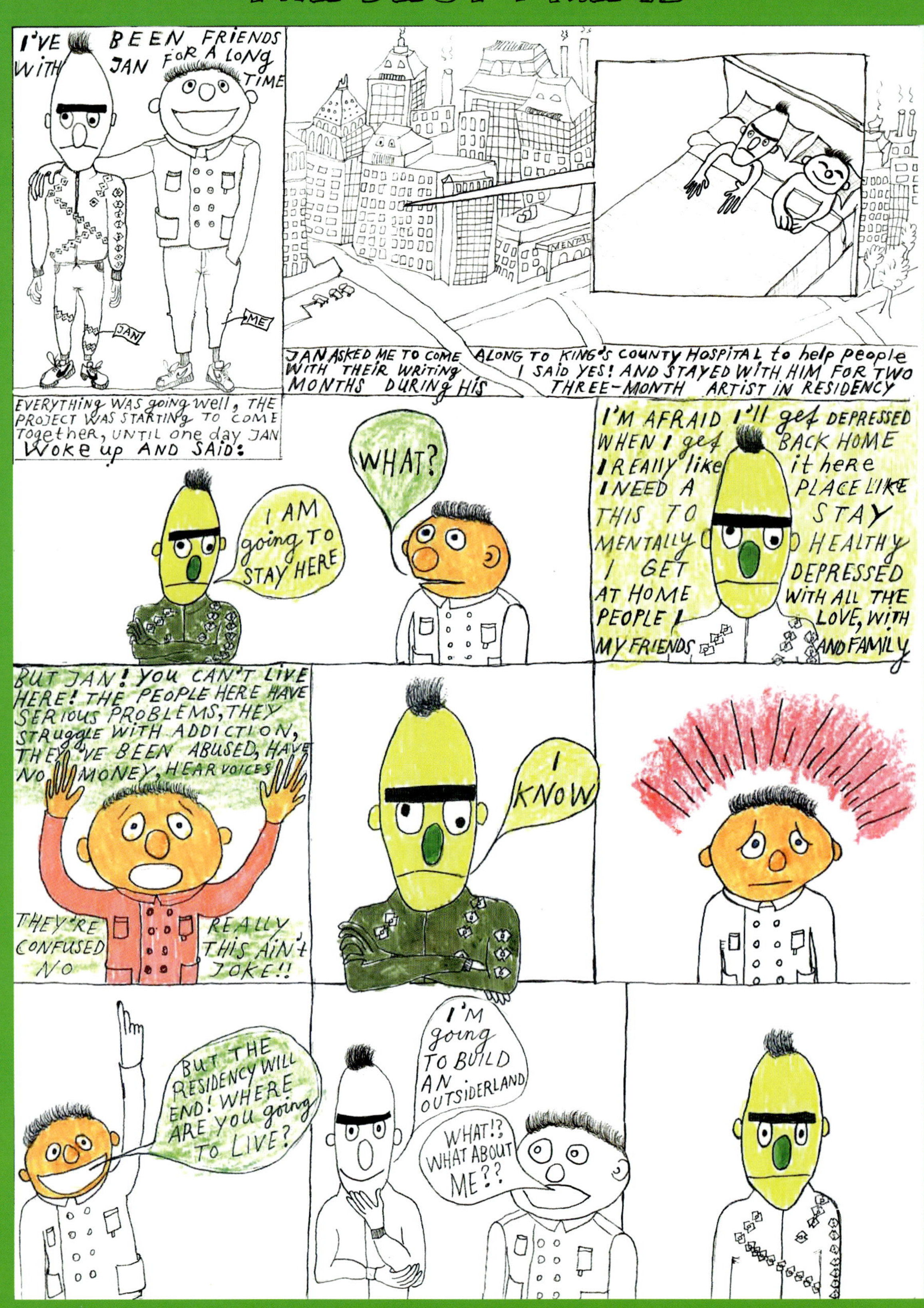

THE BEST FRIEND

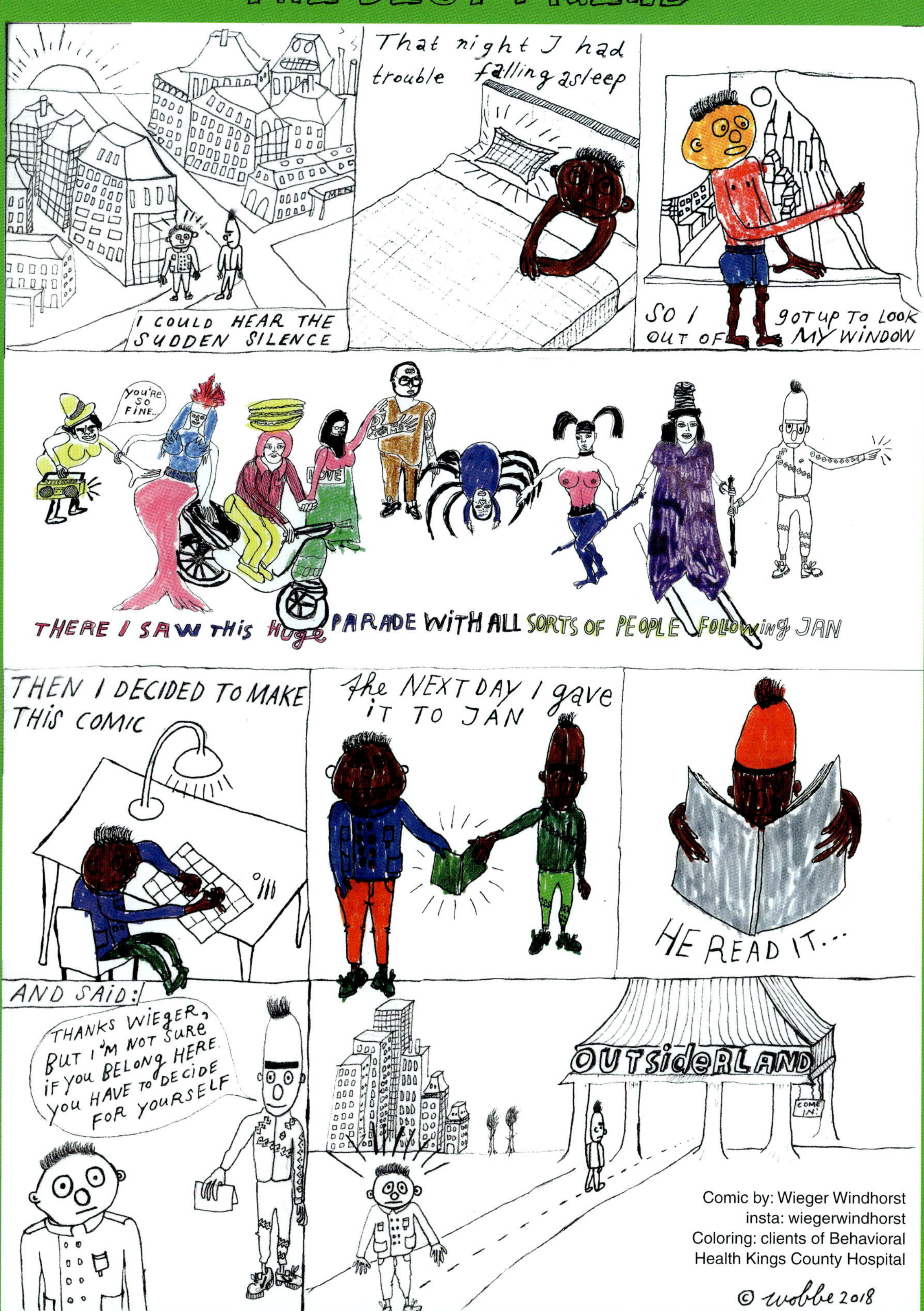

Comic by: Wieger Windhorst
insta: wiegerwindhorst
Coloring: clients of Behavioral Health Kings County Hospital

© wobbe 2018

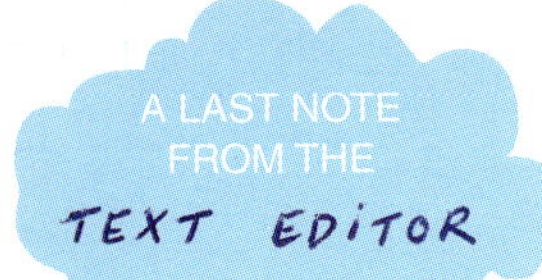

I have edited this book. I'll say it's my job, my chosen profession, and this is true. But it has filled me with some unease. There is a lie somewhere in it. Not anywhere in the book itself, nor in me, exactly. I detetect it somewhere inbetween the book and me; in the act of my work. The lie suggests itself, takes its vague shape, at the tip of my fingers as I rattle away on my keyboard, writing my corrections and suggestions. They imply an order of which the parts may be written out with certainty onto a grid with many axes, as a known quantity. There is beauty in order, in certainty, like a crystalline lattice. I like to imagine it in many things. But though the thought sooths me it's mostly an abstraction; an ideal which may be written out only ever on a surface.

I do know this lie well.

I HAVE MY OWN MADNESS; A MADNESS WHICH HAS ONLY RECENTLY BEEN GIVEN A NAME AND ITS CORRESPONDING COLLECTION OF PILLS. I SWALLOW THEM AT SET TIMES, EVERY DAY. THESE PILLS SHOULD SUBDUE THE CHAOS IN ME, AS WELL AS OTHER, MORE HARMFUL THINGS THAT LIVE IN IT. THEY WORK, TO A DEGREE. ENTHUSIASTICALLY, I HAVE SAID YES TO EVERY NEW KIND OF MEDICATION THAT HAS BEEN SUGGESTED TO ME THESE PAST FEW YEARS, BECAUSE MY MADNESS HAS BEEN WITH ME FOR A LONG TIME, SOMETIMES ONLY GURGLING BENEATH MY SHAPENED THOUGHTS, OTHER TIMES WELLING UP WILDLY, BUT NEVER TO SUBSUME MY MIND COMPLETELY. I HAVE NEVER LOST CONTROL, AND I'VE GROWN TIRED. I FIND I REGARD THE PEOPLE IN THIS BOOK WITH SOME JEALOUSY, AS IF THEY EXIST IN THEIR OWN CERTAINTY; THE OTHER EXTREME OF THAT ABSTRACT ORDER I SOMETIMES IMAGINE. THERE IS CALMNESS IN SURRENDER. AND THERE IS A LIE IN THIS TOO.

by Rens van der Knoop

OPEN THE DIALOGUE

We view the world in a way
that our message is hard to convey.
The topic that society doesn't put on display
it's a subject that even taboo stays away.
The diagnosis we put on broadway
when it's only a rough draft of a screenplay.
Its in our nature to portray the symptoms
established in our pathway.

Epiphany needs to lighten our darken hallway.
Your gifts has been downplayed,
as you can't fear your capabilities
within the doorway.

by: Jonathan, insta: jp_chase87